GROVE PRESS MODERN DRAMATISTS

Grove Press Modern Dramatists
Series Editors: *Bruce King* and *Adele King*

Published titles

Eugene Benson, *J. M. Synge*
Normand Berlin, *Eugene O'Neill*
Neil Carson, *Arthur Miller*
Ruby Cohn, *New American Dramatists, 1960–1980*
Bernard F. Dukore, *Harold Pinter*
Frances Gray, *John Arden*
Julian Hilton, *Georg Büchner*
Leonard C. Pronko, *Eugène Labiche and Georges Feydeau*
Theodore Shank, *American Alternative Theater*
Nick Worrall, *Nikolai Gogol and Ivan Turgenev*

Further titles in preparation

GROVE PRESS MODERN DRAMATISTS

NIKOLAI GOGOL and IVAN TURGENEV

Nick Worrall

Grove Press, Inc., New York

Copyright © 1983 by Nick Worrall

All Rights Reserved

No part of this book may be reproduced, stored in a retrieval system, or transmitted in any form, by any means, including mechanical, electronic, photocopying, recording, or otherwise, without the prior written permission of the publisher.

First published in 1982 by
THE MACMILLAN PRESS LTD.,
London and Basingstoke

First Evergreen Edition 1983
First Printing 1983
ISBN: 0-394-62431-9
Library of Congress Catalog Card Number: 82-82237

Printed in Hong Kong

GROVE PRESS INC.,
196 West Houston Street,
New York, N.Y. 10014

Contents

	List of Plates	vi
	Editors' Preface	vii
1	Two Lives	1
2	Two Worlds	17
3	Theatrical Theories and Influences	31
4	Gogol's Plays 1832–1842	48
5	*The Government Inspector*	81
6	Turgenev's Plays 1834–1848	116
7	Turgenev's Plays 1848–1850	139
8	*A Month in the Country*	170
	Notes and References	188
	Bibliography	194
	Editions of the Plays of Gogol and Turgenev in Translation	198
	Index	201

List of Plates

1. Marya Savina as Marya Antonovna in Gogol's *The Government Inspector*, Alexandrinski Theatre, St Petersburg, 1881
2. A scene from Act 5 of *The Government Inspector*, Moscow Art Theatre, 1908
3. Michael Chekhov as Khlestakov in *The Government Inspector*, Moscow Art Theatre, 1921
4. Erast Garin as Khlestakov in *The Government Inspector*, Meyerhold Theatre, Moscow, 1926
5. Alec Guinness as Khlestakov in *The Government Inspector*, New Theatre, London, 1948. Photograph: John Vickers
6. *L to R:* Olga Yakovleva as Agafya, Mikhail Kozakov as Kochkaryov and Nikolai Volkov as Podkolyosin in Gogol's *Marriage*, Malaya Dronnaya Theatre, Moscow, 1975
7. *L:* K. Stanislavski *and R:* V. Kachalov as Rakitin in the 1909 Moscow Art Theatre production of Turgenev's *A Month in the Country*
8. Design by M. V. Dobuzhinski for Act 1 of *A Month in the Country*, Moscow Art Theatre, 1909
9. *L to R:* Valerie Taylor as Natalya Petrovna and Isolde Denham as Vera in *A Month in the Country*, St James's Theatre, London, 1943
10. Angela Baddeley as Natalya Petrovna and Michael Redgrave as Rakitin in *A Month in the Country*, Old Vic Theatre, London, 1950
11. K. Stanislavski and his wife, M. Lilina, as Count Lyubin and Darya Ivanovna in Turgenev's *A Provincial Lady*, Moscow Art Theatre, 1912
12. L. M. Leonidov as Tropachov and L. M. Koreneva as Olga Petrovna in Turgenev's *The Parasite*, Moscow Art Theatre, 1912

Editors' Preface

The *Grove Press Modern Dramatists* is an international series of introductions to major and significant nineteenth- and twentieth-century dramatists, movements and new forms of drama in Europe, Great Britain, America and new nations such as Nigeria and Trinidad. Besides new studies of great and influential dramatists of the past, the series includes volumes on contemporary authors, recent trends in the theatre and on many dramatists, such as writers of farce, who have created theatre 'classics' while being neglected by literary criticism. The volumes in the series devoted to individual dramatists include a biography, a survey of the plays, and detailed analysis of the most significant plays, along with discussion, where relevant, of the political, social, historical and theatrical context. The authors of the volumes, who are involved with theatre as playwrights, directors, actors, teachers and critics, are concerned with the plays as theatre and discuss such matters as performance, character interpretation and staging, along with themes and contexts.

Editors' Preface

Grove Press Modern Dramatists are written for people interested in modern theatre who prefer concise, intelligent studies of drama and dramatists, without jargon and an excess of footnotes.

BRUCE KING
ADELE KING

1
Two Lives

There is a consensus of twentieth-century opinion which recognizes the greatness of Gogol and Turgenev as novelists, although for very different reasons in each case. Gogol has been rediscovered as a forerunner of the 'absurdist' school of writers, possessing a complex literary style which deconstructs and dehumanizes the world it describes while challenging our preconceptions of what constitutes 'reality' or 'humanity'. Turgenev, however, appears as the exact opposite. His lucid, realistic narrative style is seen to construct and stabilize a seemingly known world, reassuring us of its certainties through his power to create psychologically convincing characters, while reminding us, at the same time, of the inevitable transience of all things human. Life at least seems to be meaningful in Turgenev's fiction. In Gogol, the entire scheme of things appears meaningless and comically grotesque.

As a statement of the differences between the two writers, these generalizations would probably find agreement with any Western reader familiar with the first part of *Dead Souls* and *Fathers and Sons*, but could the same degree of assent be expected if the contrasts were between the plays *Marriage* and *The Parasite*? The question needs to be asked because the drama of Gogol and Turgenev has remained a neglected area in most discussions in English of their work, and is invariably treated as incidental to their main achievements in the field of the novel and short story. The plays of Gogol and Turgenev are not only as valuable, intrinsically, as their other creative work but, perhaps more importantly, must be properly appreciated if the work of each writer is to be considered as a unified whole. The differences between Turgenev and Gogol, as usually evidenced by reference to their prose writing, are not so great as they appear on the surface; as *dramatists* they both speak to the twentieth century on matters human with one voice, and with an urgency and immediacy which demands the public forum of the stage.

On 20 March 1809, Nikolai Vasilyevich Gogol-Yanovski was born in Sorochintsy in the Ukrainian province of Poltava. His parents belonged to the petty landed gentry and their ancestors were of Cossack origin. The second part of the family name, which Gogol later dropped, hints at connections with Polish aristocracy. His mother was an intensely neurotic woman who had married at fourteen and produced four other children – three sisters and a brother for the young Nikolai. His father, who seems to have had no definite occupation, had artistic pretensions and wrote comedies in Ukrainian for private performance in the mansions of the local gentry. He died in 1825 when Gogol was just sixteen and attending high school.

On 28 October 1818, Ivan Sergeyevich Turgenev was born in Spasskoye in the province of Oryol, Central Russia. His parents were well-to-do, the wealth belonging in the main to the mother, who was older than Turgenev's father, and whom he had married with a discreet eye on the property which formed part of her dowry. Another son, Nikolai, had been born two years earlier. The father was a charming, good-looking ex-officer who relished unemployed retirement and was a notorious womanizer. He died in 1834 when Turgenev was just sixteen and had enrolled in the Department of History and Philology at the University of St Petersburg.

Both Gogol and Turgenev were strongly influenced by their mothers. Turgenev's was an intelligent, fiercely feudal matriarch who is said to have used such physical violence against the servants on her estate that, in one instance, death resulted. The incident is described in Turgenev's short story *The Brigadier*. She apparently used to beat Ivan frequently. Her passionate nature, fortunately, also extended to the arts and some of her intense love for music and the stage would seem to have been inherited by her younger son. Gogol's mother was less distinguished, intellectually, than Turgenev's. She terrified her young son with tales of hell-fire and damnation, leaving indelible scars on an impressionable mind, while superstitiously believing him to be in some sense 'chosen' for higher things. Marya Ivanovna seems to have implanted this sense of his 'destiny' in her son's infant consciousness. It became a frequent topic of their later correspondence – full of grammatical errors and spelling mistakes on her part but interesting none the less. Even at school, ordinary events in Gogol's life – a cold, the award of good or bad marks – seemed to him to be tokens of a supernatural guardianship.

It is perhaps not surprising that, as a result of their childhood experiences, neither man married. Gogol seemed incapable of forming a normal relationship with the opposite sex. Turgenev, on the other hand, had many affairs, fathered an illegitimate daughter whom he cared for all his life, and formed one permanent, platonic relationship – with a married woman, Pauline Viardot-Garcia, a famous soprano who was sister to the great contralto, Malibran, prima-donna of the Italian opera in Paris during the 1820s and 1830s.

Turgenev was educated privately at a boarding school in Moscow, where his parents moved when he was nine and then, later, was tutored at home in true aristocratic fashion. Gogol went to conventional schools, first in Poltava and then, for seven years, to a high school in Nezhin. Turgenev's environment was French-speaking. He learned his Russian from the serfs on the estate. Gogol was surrounded by Russian and, of course, Ukrainian speakers on the small family estate of Vasilyevka. Gogol did not visit Europe until he was in his late teens, in 1829, and then only briefly. The first of Turgenev's many trips abroad during his youth was at the age of four, when he was taken to Switzerland and nearly fell into the bear pit at Berne. No psychological scars appear to have been left by this adventure. Gogol's early life, by contrast, appears full of material for the would-be analyst. Apart from stories of the Last Judgement told him by his mother, of a kind which sent him to church every Sunday 'in a fever of mingled adoration and dread,' [1] his grandmother regaled him with horrifying tales of the supernatural, old songs and terrifying folk-tales, the subject matter of which found its way into his early short stories. He was also prone to experiencing, while alone in the garden, what he later described as 'the agonising sensation of the void'. This is recounted as a personal aside in the story *Old World Landowners*.

The first encounter of both future writers with the wider

social world of nineteenth century Russia involved the inevitable move, for the sons of gentry, to the capital, St Petersburg; Gogol in 1828 and Turgenev in 1834. Between these dates Gogol had written, and had had published at his own expense under the pseudonym V. Alov, a narrative poem entitled *Hanz Kuechelgarten*. Critical reaction had been damning and Gogol spent the few weeks after publication buying up every available copy of the book and destroying it, evidencing a morbid degree of sensitivity to criticism which was to have disastrous consequences at a later date. He found work as a civil servant in the department of public buildings of the Ministry of the Interior, experience which was to prove invaluable when he came to compose *Diary of a Madman* and *The Overcoat*. He also auditioned as an actor at the Imperial Theatres where, overcome with nervousness, he failed miserably.

In May 1831, the first part of *Evenings on a Farm Near Dikanka* was published under Gogol's own name, containing four tales of the vaguely supernatural in a Ukrainian setting. Also, in May of that year, he met the person who exercized supreme influence on his creative output – the poet, prose writer and dramatist Alexander Pushkin. In 1832, the second part of *Evenings on a Farm Near Dikanka* appeared, containing the story *Ivan Fyodorovich Shponka and His Aunt*, which marked the advent of the authentically Gogolian literary personality and carried the hallmarks of the style which were to characterize his later masterpieces.

Gogol became passionately interested in the mediaeval period of European civilization and threw himself into the study of history. In 1831 he obtained a post as professor of history at the Patriotic Institute, a school for girls, and then had the temerity to apply for the vacant chair of history at the University of Kiev. Although he did not get the post, he was shortly afterwards, in 1834, appointed assistant professor of history at the University of St Petersburg. His opening lecture – on the Middle Ages – was very well received. It had been well prepared and Gogol had natural histrionic gifts. However, his success as a history professor was short-lived, despite the ambitiousness of some of his projects. In a letter to Pushkin he spoke of a planned multi-volume history of the Ukraine, which he had been contemplating for some time, and even spoke of a history of the world. None of this work ever saw the light of day. It is doubtful whether any of it existed except in Gogol's own imagination. His interest in history was, however, real enough and at least two of his unfinished plays, *Alfred* and *The Shaved-Off Moustache*, were intended as serious historical dramas. The extent of the doubt as to how much Gogol actually knew about history was expressed by Turgenev:

> I was one of his students in 1835 when he lectured (!) on history to us at St Petersburg University. His lecturing, to tell the truth, was highly original. In the first place, Gogol usually missed two lectures out of three; secondly, even when he appeared in the lecture room, he did not so much speak as whisper something incoherently and showed us small engravings of views of Palestine and other Eastern countries, looking terribly embarrassed all the time. We were all convinced that he knew nothing of history (and we were hardly wrong) and that Mr Gogol-Janovsky, our professor (he appeared under that name in the list of lecturers) had nothing in common with the writer Gogol . . .[2]

In 1836, while still a student in St Petersburg, Turgenev

showed *his* first literary effort – a Byronically inspired dramatic poem, *Styeno* – to the university rector, P. A. Pletnyov, who was also a poet and critic as well as a friend of Pushkin and Gogol. He had written this in 1834, at the age of sixteen, and during the following three years wrote hundreds of lyric poems as well as a drama, nameless and since lost. He also translated parts of *Othello* and *King Lear* as well as commencing his own rather precocious autobiography.

In the meantime, Gogol had become an established writer with a developing reputation. The set of short stories *Mirgorod*, in two volumes, had appeared almost simultaneously with *Arabesques*, in 1835, and in the same year he began work on *Dead Souls*, which was to preoccupy him until his death in 1852. Towards the end of 1835, armed with a suggestion from Pushkin to whom he had addressed a request for a 'subject for a comedy', he began writing *Revizor*, or *The Government Inspector*. The work was finished in a matter of weeks, was miraculously passed by the censor without any problems, and was premiered at the Alexandrinski Theatre in St Petersburg, one of the two Imperial Theatres, with the Tsar himself in attendance on 19 April 1836. Gogol had attended rehearsals and had been unhappy with the actors. Turgenev, who saw the production, described it as being acted in the traditional vaudeville manner of the time. Immediate critical reaction was harsh, although the Tsar described himself rather complacently as pleased with the play in which 'everybody got his come-uppance – me as much as anybody'. Disappointed with the performance in St Petersburg, made only slightly happier by the Moscow production and dismayed by the play's critical reception, Gogol fled abroad where he was to remain until 1848, returning to his native land on only two occasions.

Nikolai Gogol and Ivan Turgenev

The death of Pushkin in a duel, in 1837, was a bitter blow to Gogol. Pushkin, Gogol said, had given him the idea for *The Government Inspector*, had suggested the theme of *Dead Souls* to him, had talked with him on matters artistic, had listened to and commented on readings of his work. Gogol was inconsolable and some commentators have attributed his artistic decline, even his early death, to the loss of Pushkin's presence and spiritual leadership.

In May 1838, Turgenev also left Russia to continue his studies abroad. From now until his death in 1883 he, in common with Gogol, was to spend most of his years away from his native country. In 1840, he was in Berlin where he met Mikhail Bakunin, later to become a leading member of the Anarchist movement. At the time they were both studying philosophy and both were under the influence of N. V. Stankevich, spiritual leader of the Young Hegelians. Turgenev also had a spiritual interest in Bakunin's sister, Tatyana. The enthusiasm for German philosophy was widespread among the Russian intelligentsia of the day and Hegel held a prominent place. In 1843, Turgenev met for the first time the socially-conscious literary critic, V. G. Belinski, and the history of their friendship is movingly chronicled in the former's *Literary Reminiscences*. In April of the same year, Turgenev's long poem *Parasha*, written in imitation of Pushkin's *Eugene Onegin*, had appeared and in late October he was to establish the most significant female relationship of his life when he met Pauline Viardot.

Gogol spent the eight years up to 1842 writing and re-writing his play *The Government Inspector*, working on a two-act comedy, *Marriage*, and the first part of *Dead Souls*. The number of drafts which are known to exist of *Marriage* testify to Gogol's painstaking methods of composition, although some of the re-writing was rendered necessary by the demands of the censor. In 1842, *Marriage* received its first performance in St Petersburg and was shortly followed by its Moscow premiere with Gogol's one-act play *Gamblers* as a curtain raiser. Neither was a success. In November 1843, Gogol committed one of his acts of self-destruction when he burned the first version of the second part of *Dead Souls*.

Between 1846 and 1851, Turgenev worked at what many consider to be his most significant creative achievement of these years, namely the series of stories of rural life in pre-emancipation Russia entitled *A Hunter's Sketches*. One of the unfortunate consequences of this acclaim has been the undervaluation of an equally important part of Turgenev's artistic output during these years – namely most of his plays.

In January 1847, the literary journal *The Contemporary* published the first story of the *Hunter's Sketches* cycle, *Khor and Kalinich*. It is probable that in his depiction of the milieu of the Russian peasant Turgenev had been influenced by Gogol in his choice of subject matter, although their methods of treatment and their respective artistic personalities were far apart. Turgenev might not have treated the world of the peasantry in his prose if there had not been the example of Gogol before him and the same may be said of his treatment, in plays such as *Moneyless* and *The Bachelor*, of the St Petersburg world of impoverished gentry and petty officials. Nothing, however, could have better emphasized their wide disparity in sensibility, as well as social and political outlook, than the publication in 1847 of Gogol's *Selected Passages from Correspondence with Friends*. These essays' ultra-conservative view of the Nicolaevan autocracy, their sycophantic abasement before the power of the Orthodox

Nikolai Gogol and Ivan Turgenev

Church, their obscurantist notions of popular education and how the peasantry should be treated, baffled and dismayed Gogol's friends and admirers. At the time of their publication Turgenev was in Salzbrunn, where he had travelled in company with Belinski, and it was from Salzbrunn that Belinski addressed his famous *Letter to Gogol*, which subjected the author of *Selected Passages* to one of the most famous verbal lashings in literary history.

Smarting from Belinski's criticism, which he had attempted to answer but without much spirit and with many concessions, Gogol felt the need to undergo religious penance. He went on a pilgrimage to the Holy Land. Meanwhile, Europe was in revolutionary upheaval. Turgenev heard in Brussels, in February 1848, of the *coup d'état* in France and immediately hurried to Paris where he met the Russian expatriate socialist, Alexander Herzen, and Bakunin. He observed events with a detached eye and described them with artistic precision in the short story *My Mates Sent Me*. Commenting to Pauline Viardot on a day spent in the streets, he wrote: 'What is history, then? Providence, irony, or fatality?' [3] He was still in Paris in June when the red flag was raised at the barricades.

In November 1850, Turgenev's mother died and he came into his estate. He returned to Russia and spent the whole of the summer of 1851 at Spasskoye. Gogol had already returned to Moscow in 1848, and made an attempt to join in the literary life of the city. He befriended the novelist Ivan Goncharov, got to know the editor and poet N. A. Nekrasov, and went to a reading by Alexander Ostrovski of the latter's play *It's a Family Affair*. All three were also personally known to Turgenev and both he and Gogol numbered among their additional literary acquaintances the poet Mikhail Lermontov, and the novelist Fyodor Dostoevski.

Two Lives

While in Frankfurt, in July 1845, Gogol had burned a new version of the second volume of *Dead Souls* and, since 1847, had come under the influence and tutelage of a country priest, Father Matthew Konstantinovski who, according to whichever version of their relationship you feel more inclined to accept, either hounded Gogol spiritually to death (the more popular account) or gave genuine religious support to a personality already self-tormented to the point of extinction. Work on the second part of *Dead Souls*, which was to be the spiritually regenerated counterpart of the first, continued but was obviously a source of anguish. It was now that Turgenev met him face to face for the first time.

Gogol's interest in Turgenev had been aroused as early as 1846 when, in a letter of 7 September to his friend, the literary critic P. V. Annenkov, he wrote:

> Give me an idea of the young Turgenev. His talent is quite *remarkable* and promises a great deal for the future. [4]

Their mutual friend, the actor Mikhail Shchepkin, took Turgenev to meet Gogol on 20 October 1851. During an animated conversation Gogol began to speak approvingly of censorship, at which point Turgenev became aware of 'an impassable gulf between Gogol's outlook on life and mine'. At the same time, he was aware that 'a great poet, a great artist was before me and I looked at him and listened to him with veneration even when I did not agree with him.'[5]

Accounts of Gogol's final days and hours are all horrific – the self-imposed starvation, the suicidal element in his feelings of religious penitence, the burning of his manuscripts and the primitive medical attention (leeches on the nose accompanied by head-dowsings with ice-cold water). News of his final illness had been current in St Petersburg several days before his death on 21 February 1852. On 13 March, the newspaper *Moscow News* carried an obituary article by Turgenev which led to his arrest on 16 April. He had originally sent the article to a St Petersburg journal but the editor had refused to publish it because of fears of censorship. Turgenev was already under suspicion for *A Hunter's Sketches*, which had been seen as an attack on the institution of serfdom, and his friends believed that his punishment – a month in prison followed by exile to his estate under police surveillance – was not only for the obituary (in which he dared to describe a snivelling, pen-pushing neurotic as a 'great man') but was also on account of *A Hunter's Sketches*. The censor who had approved the book for publication had already been removed from his post.

The story of the remaining thirty years of Turgenev's life is one of increasing fame and success accompanied by increasing resignation and pessimism before life's disappointments and the contemplation of death. This feeling does not appear very strongly in his plays but shows itself in his prose from 1850 onwards. It may partially be seen as a consequence of the defeats of 1848 before which the libertarian spirit, and radical feeling generally, crept into its shell, buried its dead or licked its wounds, while the middle classes of Europe celebrated their triumph. Turgenev, like his friend and fellow-writer, Leo Tolstoy, was an aristocrat with little sympathy for the class which the French and Industrial Revolutions had brought to power. On the other hand, while sympathizing with the plight of worker and peasant, neither favoured political and social revolution. The true nature of the 1861 emancipation, for example, must have struck Turgenev with

Two Lives

forceful irony, as his novel *Virgin Soil* to an extent reveals when, rather than serving as a mechanism of liberation, the emancipating legislation provided cheap migrant labour to staff the emergent factory system. Turgenev, believing in neither the structure of the past nor the apparent form of the future, lived on in eminence and disillusionment.

In 1855, Turgenev had written *Rudin* at a time when he was already beginning to consider himself a spent literary force. In the same year some of his *Hunter's Sketches* were published by Dickens in the magazine *Household Words*. These translations had been preceded by the publication in England in the previous year of *Dead Souls*, with the curious title *Home Life in Russia*. In August 1856, Turgenev visited Alexander Herzen in London from where the latter had been editing and distributing copies of the radical socialist journal *Kolokol* (The Bell) for secret transportation into Russia. Nicholas I, the 'gendarme of Europe', had died the previous year and there was hope that the regime of Alexander II would be less harsh and repressive. Turgenev was in London again in May 1857, when he made the acquaintance of Carlyle, Thackeray, Disraeli and Macaulay.

In 1859, his novel *A Nest of Gentlefolk* (sometimes translated as *Liza*) was published and, in February of the following year, *On the Eve* appeared. In August 1861, during a visit to England, he made a trip to the Isle of Wight where he first had the idea for his most famous novel, *Fathers and Sons*, which describes the conflict between the generations of the 1860s and 1840s represented, on the one hand by the nihilist Bazarov and his friend Arkadi, and on the other by the Anglophile Pavel and Arkadi's father. During the previous year he had delivered a speech in St Petersburg on the theme of

Nikolai Gogol and Ivan Turgenev

'Hamlet and Don Quixote'. The dual natures represented by the active and combative – as opposed to the passive and contemplative – types, which these two characters appeared to him to personify, had always struck Turgenev as archetypal.

In January 1863, he was accused of being involved with what became known as the 'Affair of the 32' in connection with the distribution of anti-Russian propaganda in London. He was summoned to St Petersburg to testify to the nature of his connections with Alexander Herzen and *The Bell* and was subsequently absolved, although what Herzen considered to be Turgenev's mealy-mouthed version of his relationship with the radicals caused a rift between them. Bakunin was especially scathing.

Turgenev took up permanent residence in London in November 1870, and from across the Channel contemplated the political events of the Paris Commune the following year. In July 1871, he indulged in a little aristocratic hunting and shooting on a Scottish estate near Pitlochry (he was a passionate sportsman for most of his life) and he also took part in the Sir Walter Scott centenary celebrations in Edinburgh. While in Scotland he met Robert Browning whom he did not much like. He admired the poetry of Swinburne and the novels of George Eliot, whom he met in 1878. He considered D. G. Rossetti 'decadent'. Apart from his fondness for Dickens he appears to have had no other particularly strong feelings about contemporary English literature.

In October 1871, he moved to Paris. There he established a close relationship with Gustave Flaubert, and the famous literary dinners of 'The Five' as they were called – Flaubert, Turgenev, Daudet, Zola and Goncourt – date from the mid-seventies. Turgenev was already well known in French literary circles, not only through translations of his work but through his acquaintance with Prosper Mérimée, Victor Hugo, Guy de Maupassant, George Sand and others.

His last major work, the novel *Virgin Soil*, was published in 1876 and, in August 1878, he returned to Russia for a short visit, staying for a while with Leo Tolstoy at the latter's country estate. An earlier quarrel between the two men had almost led to a duel, so the reconciliation was very much welcomed by both. In the relaxed atmosphere of the Tolstoy home, Turgenev indulged in one of his favourite pastimes of amateur theatricals and charades. One of his forfeits was to dance the can-can. Tolstoy noted in his diary: 'Turgenev. Can-Can. Sad.' One of Turgenev's last acts was to write a letter to Tolstoy from his deathbed, urging him to return to the kind of literary work represented by *War and Peace* and *Anna Karenina* which, by this time, Tolstoy had pronounced worthless.

Meanwhile, honours continued to mount. He was elected vice-president of an international literary congress in Paris, in 1878, with Victor Hugo as president. On his return to Russia in January 1879, for the funeral of his brother Nikolai, he was paid nation-wide homage and, in June of the same year, he was notified that an honorary degree of Doctor of Civil Law had been conferred on him by the University of Oxford. The ceremony was held on 18 June, following which he travelled to London where he met Henry James.

In 1880, Turgenev was in St Petersburg for the celebrations in honour of Pushkin's jubilee and attended the unveiling of a Pushkin monument in Moscow. At the latter ceremony he made a speech which was effective enough but was completely overshadowed by one given by Dostoevski. Turgenev had first met the author of *Crime and Punishment* in 1845, and in 1860 they had together taken part in a benefit performance of Gogol's *The Government Inspector*. They met again in Germany in 1867, and quarrelled over Turgenev's novel *Smoke*. This dispute led to thinly disguised satirical portraits of Turgenev appearing in Dostoevski's novels (Karmazinov in *The Possessed* for example). However, before Dostoevski's death in January 1881, they had effected a partial reconciliation.

In the twilight of his life, in 1879, aged 61, Turgenev attended a revival of his play *A Month in the Country* and saw the young Marya Savina in the role of Verochka. Turgenev fell in love with the young actress just as the ageing Ibsen had become infatuated with Emilie Bardach in an apparent psychological attempt at rejuvenation.

In May 1883, Pauline's husband Louis Viardot died but by now Turgenev had been ill for a year with the cancer of the spine which was to kill him. He died on 22 August at Bougival in the country house near Paris which he and Pauline had jointly purchased in 1874. A memorial service was held at the Gare du Nord before his body was transported to St Petersburg where it was interred at the Volkovo cemetery – the burial place of many of Russia's great writers.

2
Two Worlds

The world which Turgenev and Gogol entered at the beginning of the nineteenth century was rapidly changing. The process which was taking place in Russia can be compared with what was happening in England during Shakespeare's lifetime. Russia at the end of the nineteenth century was, like Britain at the turn of the sixteenth, between two worlds – between feudalism and capitalism, between one sense of identity and another, between native traditions and those more broadly European, between a sense (somewhat idealized) of community and one of assertive individualism.

The process which had led to this historical conjuncture can be said to have been accelerated by the actions of Peter the Great at the beginning of the eighteenth century. Aware of the extent to which Russia, nominally a European country, remained wrapped in mediaeval obscurity, he resolved to precipitate her, by decree if necessary, out of the past and into the present. The trauma of this accelerated process can be imagined. It only needs to be compared with the feverishly accelerated pace of social change chronicled by the Elizabethans in their time. The European gates of Russia were thrown open and through them poured, in undifferentiated confusion, art, literature, architecture, science, politics, philosophy, capital, machinery – all mingling and interacting with a culture which had survived, virtually unchanged, since the Dark Ages. One important consequence of the ferment caused by the meeting of these two cultures was the unprecedented flowering of literature, music and the arts which occurred in Russia from the 1750s onwards.

Almost overnight, the literatures of Ancient Greece, of the English and Spanish Renaissances, of seventeenth-century France and eighteenth-century Germany, appeared and were devoured wholesale and indiscriminately by a nation starved for centuries of everything which passes for culture in the Western world. Devoured by only a select few, of course. Russia's intensely feudal social structure had produced a very unbalanced system where those who could read and write and who owned property and wealth were proportionately outnumbered by those who could do neither by about 99 to 1. It took another traumatic experience in the twentieth century to reverse that polarity.

The 'westernization' of Russia continued apace throughout the eighteenth-century. The 'free-thinking' ideas of Voltaire even appealed to the Empress Catherine, whilst she simultaneously sanctioned the bloody repression of the peasant rebellion led by Pugachov. Another product of those same free-thinking ideas, the French Revolution, serving as it did to spark off revolutionary ideas rather nearer home, was too close for comfort. Peter's social reforms had led not only to the creation of a whole bureaucratic structure, ranged in a

Two Worlds

'Table of Ranks' to staff the Europeanization plan. ('In Moscow you seldom see an official button on a coat; in Petersburg there is not a coat without official buttons,' wrote Gogol); [1] it also led to the emergence of a discreet class of intelligentsia, owing no loyalty except to the world of ideas, whose radical leaders, committed to the idea of social service and social change, saw an entrenched feudal monarchy as inimical to this principle.

Russia's physical precipitation into Europe was brought about by Napoleon's invasion in 1812. Had either Catherine or Alexander I wished to halt the process of Europeanization, the invasion, followed by Russia's military success, ironically had the opposite effect. Napoleon's defeat brought the Russian presence geographically into Europe, as Alexander's armies pursued the retreating French to the gates of Paris. Russia was now a major European power as well as a determinedly reactionary one, resolved to stamp out any revolutionary sparks at home and abroad. The incarnation of this aggressive spirit of oppression proved to be Alexander I's successor, his son Nicholas, who turned his country into a barracks staffed by spies and informers, which he ruled 'methodically and ruthlessly, unmoved by either flattery or abuse'[2]. Any attempt at free expression was stamped out; opposition was stifled.

A remarkable, and seemingly contradictory, fact of this age of oppression is that it failed to stifle, despite censorship and other measures, the intensely vigorous growth of literary and artistic activity. The years of Nicholas's reign, 1825–55, were those when Gogol completed his entire literary *oeuvre*, while Turgenev produced a substantial proportion of his total literary output, including all of his plays. Pushkin produced some of his greatest work during this period, including his novel in verse,

Nikolai Gogol and Ivan Turgenev

Eugene Onegin. Lermontov was also creatively active as were Goncharov and Dostoevski. It was a truly 'Golden Age' in the history of Russian literature, formed by the dialectic between the forces of the State and the historical process, a conflict which is reflected in the creative work of the period.

There are a number of preoccupations which both Gogol and Turgenev share, emanating from the world in which they found themselves. They express a concern for the structure of a past society which represented some form of ideal, usually Ancient Greece. Together with this goes a nostalgia for an organic culture, a Golden Age of social indivisibility. Although this feeling tends to be sentimental, it is related to what both see as the development of a new meaning of 'individual' as aspirant, self-seeking, indifferent to the mass, economically aggressive or intellectually aloof.

There is a tendency, more pronounced on Gogol's part, to idealize the past and to fear the process of change. The focus of idealization apart from classical Greece, tends to be the Middle Ages. His uncompleted play about the Anglo-Saxon king, Alfred the Great, seems an attempt to recreate dramatically the ideal of a former heroism of semi-mythological proportions and representative of an age whose lore was commensurate with the creative powers of its people. This state of affairs is contrasted, by implication, with the feebleness on a human level, as well as the poverty of imagination, of contemporary society. Gogol shares some of the feeling which characterised William Morris, John Ruskin and the English pre-Raphaelites in their attempts to oppose the process of industrialization, with its fragmenting effects on human relationships, epitomized by the imposition of the division of labour. Gogol's world is often artistically represented

Two Worlds

as a whirl of incoherent and unconnected fragments, in which there is little distinction between people and objects and through which his intense concern with a feeling of human and social breakdown can be felt. The feeling is less intense in Turgenev and the effect is less nightmarish, grotesque and absurd. Nevertheless, the intuition that life is somehow insubstantial, dream-like, having the unreality of play, can be seen as a response to this confusion and is also a tribute, in part, to Calderon, for whose work (especially *Life is a Dream*) Turgenev felt an abiding admiration.

Both Gogol and Turgenev were very much influenced by eighteenth- and nineteenth-century German philosophy. Whereas Turgenev made an intensive study of philosophy while a student at the University of Berlin, there is no clear-cut evidence that Gogol made any special study or came under the influence of any particular member of the German school. He was a romantic idealist in the Hegelian mould to the extent that he was aware of an eternal dialectic between spirit and matter, between the imaginative aspirant world of the ideal and the downward tug of reality. He sought, through an art which depicted the baseness of that reality, to transform it and, simultaneously, to bring about the spiritual regeneration of his readers. His art had a semi-divine mission. For Gogol there was no kind of social transformation which could be brought about through the application of practical, materialist means, through economics or through social revolution. The only possible revolution was spiritual.

Gogol considered that the forms of Greek life, its literature and its art, represented an ideal towards which contemporary Russia should be striving. His view of ancient civilization provided the basis for a critique of the present which, he claimed, lacked precisely that ideal harmony and unity. The dream of the past had vanished but it could be resurrected by the thought of the poet. It was as a poet that Gogol thought of himself. Paradise could be regained, and it is no accident that Gogol called his contemporary 'Odyssey' (*Dead Souls*) a *poema*, having in mind the Greek epic form on which it is based and in which he occasionally either parodies or adopts the true epic strain. Gogol believed in the strength to dream. His early short stories are packed with folklore, paying tribute to the exuberant power of the irrational and the subconscious.

Turgenev also revered the Greek world, although he had no programme as such for its reconstitution in the present. He preferred, as he put it, 'the wide sky of the ancients' and shared their pagan inclination to identify the Deity with Nature. As a young man he steeped himself in the study of Greek drama and worshipped the artistic worlds of Homer, Goethe and Shakespeare, the last of whom he considered the 'most human' as well as, interestingly, the 'most anti-Christian' of writers.[3]

According to Turgenev, Russians were living in a 'desolate interregnum'. While under the influence of Nikolai Stankevich, Turgenev had accepted his interpretation of Hegel, whereby contemplation was regarded as an attitude spiritually superior to one of active engagement with the world – Hamlet as a superior being to Don Quixote. Gradually, under the influence of Vissarion Belinski, who first shared these views and then abandoned them in a fit of disgust in favour of active contention with social reality, Turgenev's ground also shifted, but never from one extreme to the other. Instead he remained forever poised, swayed first one way and then the other, between these two modes of being and consciousness, emotionally biased towards the world of intervention, while intellectually realizing the grounds for passivity and contemplation.

Gogol may also be said to have shared the views of the young Belinski at a time when the latter accepted the Hegelian tenet that everything which was real was rational, that 'autocracy was, coming when it did, sacred; that Russia as it was was a part of a divine scheme marching towards an ideal goal. . .'.[4] Gogol remained convinced of Russia's divine mission and supported the status quo, which he conceived in the light of his innate idealism so that the very forces – autocracy, orthodoxy, serfdom – which, from one perspective were producing the conditions he railed against, became converted into temporarily distorted, but permanent ideals.

Turgenev was more inclined to confront reality head-on, even if he considered attempts to change it, finally, fruitless. His view of Russia in the 1840s could easily be mistaken for that of a social activist:

> You looked round: bribery was rampant, serfdom remained as firm as a rock, the barracks were in the foreground of everything, no courts of justice, rumours about the impending closure of the universities, the number of admissions to which were soon to be reduced to three hundred, journeys abroad were becoming impossible, no decent book could be ordered from abroad, a sort of dark cloud was constantly hanging over the whole of the so-called department of learning and literature and, to cap it all, denunciations whispered and spread on all sides; no common bond among the younger generation, no common interests, everyone afraid and grovelling – you might as well give it up![5]

Nikolai Gogol and Ivan Turgenev

One could not be blind to the fact that between 1825 and 1854 there were officially noted 674 peasant uprisings and 173 cases of murder of estate owners or their managers. The recognition of this state of affairs underlies *A Hunter's Sketches*.

The contrasting attitudes of Gogol and Turgenev to the European events of 1848 are instructive. There is little doubt that, despite his comparative detachment from the turbulent events which surrounded him, Turgenev awaited optimistically some positive consequences to the revolutionary events. His close association with the radicals, including Herzen and Bakunin, even his friendship with the young Dostoevski of the Petrashevski circle, a group of radicals suppressed by Nicholas I in 1849, can lead to no other assumption. By contrast, the revolutions of 1848 seemed to Gogol to betoken the complete collapse of human society.

Turgenev, with the Herzens in Paris, was typically divided in his response between recognition of the tragic nature of the events themselves, the aspirations embodied in those events, and an awareness of their illusory, theatrical air. As with all tragic moments in the world of his fiction, they similarly began to take on the forms and shapes of the world of play, where tragedy is prone to be undercut by comedy and what seems real is simultaneously shown as illusion. As an explanation of the underlying causes of Turgenev's deepening pessimism, Irving Howe's comment appears apposite:

> Turgenev wrote in the post-1848 epoch, after the failure of the last purely democratic revolutions on the continent. The 'twilight aura' that hangs like a softly pencilled cloud over his work is a reflection, to be sure, of a private condition; but it also has its source in the

feeling of hopelessness which overwhelmed many Russian intellectuals during the 1850s.[6]

Gogol, in a letter, pronounced: 'I have always avoided politics . . .It is not the poet's job to worm his way into the worldly market place'.[7]

Gogol's comparative apoliticism is additionally reflected in the negligible extent to which he participated in one of the key debates of the day – that between the Slavophiles and the Westernizers. Gogol felt himself to be, if not exactly neutral, then above the battle, his mind focused on higher things. Logically, everything about the Slavophile argument should have appealed to him – the opposition to western influence in Russia; the support for the religion of the Orthodox Church; the defence of the monarchy; the pride in indigenous customs and traditions as opposed to the supposed 'decadence' of the West. The spirit of *Selected Passages*, for example, is very much in tune with that of the Slavophiles and Gogol's views did, in fact, become part of the armoury of the more militant adherents of the faith. By contrast, the Westernizers, amongst whom Turgenev was a noted moderate, firmly believed in the modernization of the country and the conversion of autocracy into parliamentary democracy. The reason for Russia's backwardness, according to the movement's proselytizers, lay in its separation from the main currents of European political and social development. According to Herzen:

> The future of the country lies not in the resurrection of Byzantine prejudices or pseudo-national smugness but in free thought, science, individual and collective liberty, and the transformation of the social and economic order.[8]

Nikolai Gogol and Ivan Turgenev

Two themes constitute a permanent refrain in the work of both Gogol and Turgenev – Nature and Woman. Turgenev once wrote to the French moralist and orientalist, Ernest Renan, about what he termed the 'Machiavellianism' of Nature. What he was referring to was the way in which human life is subject to the laws of Nature and yet the world of Nature remains somehow apart from and alien to man. Man becomes an unnatural excrescence in an otherwise truly 'natural' world in which his physical 'nature' is constantly at odds with his intellectual self, where the weakness of his constitution makes mock of his grandiose schemes and where the scale and power of the natural world dwarfs him into insignificance. Nature constitutes a permanent backdrop to the imaginative worlds of Gogol and Turgenev, and the way in which the world of Nature is treated is never incidental but always central to the depiction of the human inhabitants of the landscape. Alongside the contrast between the natural world and the human world there is, in Turgenev's case, an accompanying belief in a form of fatalistic determinism which binds mankind to an inexorable, unbreakable pattern. Gogol too seizes on these natural patterns or cycles, and succeeds in finding in their human counterparts only repetition, habit, sameness and banality.

The way out of this impasse is through the transcendental powers of creation or through love of the feminine ideal. In his treatise on *Woman*, written either at school or as a young man and which is part story and part parable set in Ancient Greece, Gogol gives these words to Plato:

> Woman is to be forgiven everything, for her beauty reflects the divine idea of the beautiful on earth. Through her, Man is inspired to great deeds; she impels the artist to create; she is the mitigating force, the

conciliatory beam of light in this harsh world which would go to ruin without this divine, spiritual beauty.[9]

Plato goes on to assert woman's superiority in three areas:

> In beauty, she is more perfect than man; in the arts she provides the most elevated subject that any artist may want to depict; and in love, she puts man in contact with his original divine essence.[10]

There are more 'divine' women in the world of Gogol's art than there are in that of Turgenev, whose women, whilst usually spiritually superior to the men, tend at the same time to be practical, more sensual, and down-to-earth. The notion of 'the eternal feminine' nevertheless persists as an ideal and as a form incarnated in the artist. For Turgenev, the highest value is contained in the cult of beauty through art, especially in music. Unquenchable beauty appears to him in the image of a loving woman and in creativity. His feeling for Pauline Viardot seems a compound of all these elements.

Gogol has been compared with Balzac in the extent to which, although an ideological supporter of autocracy and defender of feudalism, his work can be seen as a 'progressive' critique of everything he ostensibly holds dear. This process is detectable in *Dead Souls*, although the novel lacks a completed second part in which a morally revitalized status quo was to prove the counterpart to the degenerate feudal panorama of Part One. It might be argued that Gogol failed artistically to realize the positive aspects of feudalism in his work because he sensed their unrealizability. The dialectical process becomes enshrined in the novel itself. Instead of the displacement of a negative (Part One) by a positive (Part Two), we are presented with a conflict between two negatives, between the shape of feudal Russia on the one hand and the personification of an emerging economic and social system, in the shape of Chichikov, on the other. He is the apotheosis of the entrepreneurial spirit whose very training has been in the new mode of acquisitive, individualistic, economic self-seeking.

In his other major work, *The Government Inspector*, a similar kind of opposition occurs. The world of the Russian provinces can be seen to stand for Old Russia and, just as Chichikov represented the new values which are eroding that crumbling structure, so Khlestakov represents that nullity of value before which a defunct (because spiritless in Gogol's terms) system is prepared in superstitious terror to abase and demean itself.

In *Marriage*, Gogol depicts the world of the emerging class of petty bourgeois bureaucrats, clerks and small merchants whose lives are centred on the city – in this case St Petersburg. The truth of the city for Gogol has little to do with Rastrelli's sumptuous Italianate architecture, transplanted by decree from eighteenth-century Italy to a swampy and mosquito-infested site on the edge of the Baltic. It has, instead, to do with the underlying reality of the forms of economic life which are emerging into dominance – the world of the government civil servant created by Peter's 'Table of Ranks', the commercialism and the absurdity of the pace of life where nothing has any permanence or true value, especially in the world of human relations.

Gamblers demonstrates the nightmare which human relations have become under these conditions, as well as the nightmare of a darker, pre-conscious world of devils, death and destruction which the old order and the old consciousness could harmoniously, if primitively, contain and negotiate but which the new order can only suppress or rationalize out of existence. There is a protest in Gogol's work at the forcible imposition of the manacles of reason, at the mechanical worship of cause and effect, profit and loss. He would have his devils with tails and horns, not nonentities in uniform.

Turgenev also turns his attention to the kinds of social world which are both dominant and emergent. *A Hunter's Sketches* is an exposé of the evils of the system of serfdom. He dramatizes the clash between the old and the new – never in any simplistically oppositional confrontation between positive and negative forces but where the *fact* of conflict is shown to be an inevitable part of a process. This is especially true in the novels, which are more pessimistically determinist in outlook than the earlier plays. Bazarov, in *Fathers and Sons*, emerges less as the hero of a conflict in which his progressive views are shown to triumph over those of his rivals, than as a human victim in an ultimately meaningless conflict over which Nature presides with indifference.

This feeling of fatalism cannot be said to characterize the world of his plays, with the major exception of *A Month in the Country* which Turgenev rendered more 'novel-like' in the revisions of the 1850s and 60s. Because of the close relationship of the plays' subject-matter to specific forms of economic and social life, the nature of the determinism has more clearly defined sources. This is especially true of the best plays, *The Bachelor* and *The Parasite*, the first of which deals with the close-knit world of St Petersburg petty officialdom with its caricaturing of imported bourgeois values, its snobbery and charade of human relationships. At the same time, in revealing the negative side, Turgenev manages to demonstrate a positive, through a sensitive investigation and subtle delineation of human personality in which the existence of intrinsically human values becomes defined through the depiction of their absence.

Above all, Turgenev is an essentially experimental dramatist. Each of his plays is an experiment in form and reveals differing sides of his creative personality as it developed in the climate of the 1840s and 50s.

3
Theatrical Theories and Influences

There was no professional theatre in Russia before the 1750s. By contrast, the first professional theatre in England had been established in 1576. But just as there had been dramatic activity of both secular and religious kinds before this date in England, so there was in Russia. This activity went back to ceremonies associated with the seasonal cycles, sowing and harvesting, with fertility rituals and wedding ceremonies, as well as actual performances associated with specific church holidays. There was also the tradition of the wandering minstrel, or *skomorokh*, who combined the singing of songs and playing of instruments with clowning and horseplay. As in mediaeval Europe, church rituals and drama were often closely linked. A play of *The Burning Fiery Furnace*, borrowed from the Greek Orthodox Church, is recorded as having been performed in Novgorod in the mid-sixteenth century.

The first organized *theatrical* presentation in Russia took place in 1672, when Johann Gottfried Gregori staged a play based on the Book of Esther. Tsar Alexei Mikhailovich, who commanded the performance, is said to have sat, amazed, for a total of ten hours demanding repeated performances of the work. In 1702, by decree of Peter the Great, a theatre of wood was constructed in Red Square, Moscow, and legislation was passed encouraging people to attend performances. During the next thirty years, Russians were introduced to foreign troupes who presented productions of plays by Corneille, Racine and Molière. Companies from Italy introduced them to Commedia dell'Arte and, in 1735, to their first taste of opera.

Peter the Great's daughter, who subsequently became the Empress Elizaveta Petrovna, attempted to establish a national theatre by substituting Russian actors for foreigners; in 1752 she summoned to court the company founded in 1750, in Yaroslavl, by Fyodor Volkov (1729–63), subsequently known as 'the father of the Russian theatre'. The first company of Russian actors established under royal patronage came into existence in St Petersburg in 1756. They were headed by Alexander Sumarokov (1717–77), the first native Russian dramatist of significance, who wrote both tragedies and comedies, the former based on episodes from Russian history and constructed according to the neo-classical tenets of Boileau and the French school. Comic plots were borrowed from foreign sources, in particular Molière. The repertoire during the late eighteenth century was dominated by Western European products and included sentimental comedy, adaptations of Shakespeare, and the melodramas of Kotzebue, a German who lived in Russia for some years.

The eighteenth century saw the simultaneous development of provincial and serf theatres. The latter were built on the private estates of wealthy individuals who drew their companies of actors, singers and dancers from the ranks of their own peasantry. Many great performers were discovered in this way; one of the greatest became a close friend of both Gogol and Turgenev – the actor M. S. Shchepkin (1788–1863). With the founding of the first school for the training of actors, in 1779, a rapid improvement took place in performance standards and the first of a galaxy of first-rate artists began to emerge.

Conditions were ripe for the creation of an indigenous repertoire capable of translating the unique conditions which prevailed in Russia into viable dramatic form and of displacing the pale imitations of foreign examples which a talented amateur such as Prince A. A. Shakhovskoy had popularized. A new, distinctively Russian, dramatic voice was first heard in the work of Denis Fonvizin and Alexander Griboyedov.

Denis Fonvizin (1744–92) is best known for his comedies *The Brigadier* and *The Minor*. In the former, the theme of 'gallomania', already popular in Russian literature, received its most successful treatment. Sumarokov had written comedies about the Frenchified fop who depises everything Russian but nothing hitherto quite matched the portrayals of Ivanushka and the Councillor's wife in Fonvizin's play. The remainder of the characters are stock types but they are given individual features and a brand of idiomatic language which was quite new in Russian drama and which was to influence Fonvizin's successors. *The Minor* described by Gorky as the first play in the 'critical realist' school, is aimed at the abuses of serfdom, the coarseness and ignorance of landowners, the corruption of the courts and the deleterious effects of education. As in *The Brigadier*, Fonvizin presents the conventional pair of lovers in the French style of Molière, but the main interest of the play lies in the satiric portrayal of the symbolically named types – Mrs Prostakova (Simpleton), a part acted by Gogol at school, and her brother Skotinin (Beastly), the grotesque tutors, and the spoilt infant, Mitrofan, the subject of the play.

Alexander Griboyedov (1795–1829) is principally remembered for his comedy *Woe from Wit*, sometimes translated as *The Misfortune Of Being Clever*, or *Chatski*. The play is written according to neo-classical tenets and combines colloquial diction with rhymed verse. It is a swingeing satirical attack on Muscovite high society of the 1820s as seen through the eyes of a young radical, Chatski, who returns to the metropolis from abroad. His renewed encounters with erstwhile friends and acquaintances, including his beloved Sophie, take on the alienated perspective of someone who is now a potential revolutionary. His criticism of society, which he confides naïvely and indiscriminately to all and sundry, leads to his being slandered as a madman. With the notable exception of *Woe from Wit*, comic drama tended to be 'conservative' – that is, social abuses were shown to relate less to a whole system than to the moral deficiencies or behavioural excesses of particular individuals which, by the end of the play, had been put right.

The tradition which descends to Gogol and Turgenev includes significant plays such as V. V. Kapnist's *The Slanderer* (1796), aimed at the world of the judiciary, which, as well as being considered one of the best comedies of the period, is also thought to represent a decisive advance towards the achievement marked by *The Government Inspector*. Kapnist took his example from Ya. B. Knyazhnin, who was mainly a tragedian but also turned his hand to comedies dealing, in the main, with the abuses of serfdom and criticizing members of the nobility. Knyazhnin was a Ukrainian and a friend of Gogol's father.

Theatrical Theories and Influences

Vaudeville influenced the work of both Gogol and Turgenev. It was the most popular form of dramatic entertainment in Russia during the first half of the nineteenth century, as can be seen from the fact that the number of vaudeville pieces presented annually at the Alexandrinski Theatre increased from 41, in the season 1832/3, to 149 by 1852/3. Gogol's and Turgenev's plays would frequently be performed, sandwich fashion, between two vaudeville pieces. The vaudevilles of I. A. Krylov (1768–1844) are examples of the genre. A typical plot would revolve around the difficulties faced by a pair of lovers and the way in which they coped with obstacles placed in the path of their happiness. The plots were often based on anecdotes and included satirical depictions of contemporary types, interspersed with songs and rhyming puns. One reason for their popularity was the increasing number of benefit performances for actors and the need for a play to be specially written for the occasion. Because they were so easily tossed off, vaudevilles fitted the bill perfectly.

Both Gogol and Turgenev judged the genre very severely but neither was above exploiting the resources of vaudeville in their respective ways. For example, in Krylov's *A Lesson for Daughters*, one of the characters gives himself out to be the Marquis Glagol (the Marquis of Verb). Not only does this anticipate *The Government Inspector*, but Gogol is known to have acted in the play at school. The vaudeville influence descends via Gogol to Turgenev. It can be sensed in his first play *Indiscretion*, ostensibly a serious drama, in which he parodies the conventional devices of the serenading lover who climbs walls and balconies in pursuit of his beloved but also as part of an attempt to escape the irate attentions of an ageing husband. The plot owes something to the comedies of Molière in this respect. In *Moneyless*, the hero escapes the attentions of his creditors by constantly disappearing behind a screen, popping his head out and commenting on the proceedings, until a girl from the laundry arrives, at which point he abandons his hiding place and assumes the role of gigolo. The quarrel between brother and sister over the divisions of the family estate, in *Lunch with the Marshal of the Nobility*, contains strong traces of the despised vaudeville form. Political and social satire were nothing new in vaudeville, having been introduced by F. A. Koni (1809–79) and, in the vaudeville of the 1840s, the former principal subjects for satirical treatment, the nobility, were being replaced by small landowners, merchants and clerks.

The tradition of the puppet show influenced both Gogol and Turgenev. In Gogol's case there is a special debt to the Ukrainian *vertep*, which was a two-level, portable wooden puppet booth used primarily for nativity plays, the upper level being reserved for the religious story and the lower level for farcical interludes. The booth was worked by a single operator employing glove puppets, with the result that 'two-handed' scenes tended to be the norm – something which was later typical of Ukrainian folk comedy. The tradition which descends to Gogol is more closely connected with the 'lower' level of farcical *intermezzi* in which stock characters were, for example, 'the devil', 'the boastful Pole' and 'the daring Cossack'. The characters had comic names, often verging on the obscene, and the plays were full of topical allusions. Gogol's father wrote plays very much in this popular tradition, two of which were *The Simpleton* and *The Tricks of a Woman Outwitted by a Soldier*.

The figure of Mikhail Shchepkin links Gogol and Turgenev. Not only was he a friend, but he performed in their plays, acted as an intelligent critic of their work and, through the exercise of his professional role as an actor, pursued those theatrical reforms which made possible the kind of realism desired by both writers. He was the first to emphasize the importance of rehearsal and ensemble playing. He introduced a new degree of seriousness into the art of acting, which was subsequently to influence the theories of Stanislavski. He turned the Maly Theatre, in Moscow, into a cultural institution in accordance with his belief that: 'To the actor the theatre is a temple. It is his sanctuary.' In Herzen's opinion Shchepkin 'created truth on the Russian stage; he was the first to become non-theatrical in the theatre.'[1] He also cemented ties between the theatre and the academic world through his friendships with most of the outstanding playwrights, poets and intellectuals of the day.

Through censorship, the government exercised control over the serious theatre while vaudeville and melodrama were encouraged because of their innocuous powers of distraction. Many of the finest plays of the age were not permitted performance during the lifetime of their creators, including Pushkin's *Boris Godunov*, Lermontov's *Masquerade* and *Woe from Wit*. A defence of the censor's role was offered with devastating frankness by the reactionary writer, F. Bulgarin, when he wrote, in 1826, that censorship's chief function was to direct the active attention of genuinely enlightened people towards subjects chosen by the government and that plays, as well as journalistic articles about them, should remain weapons in the hands of the government for the direction of minds according to its dictates.[2] The first censorship law had been passed in 1804 when the government gained complete control of the stage in both Moscow and St Petersburg where the Imperial Theatres had something of the status of the Patent Theatres, Drury Lane and Covent Garden, after 1737, in England. The Imperial Theatre monopoly over drama was endorsed in 1827 and, in 1842, all provincial troupes and their repertoires came under government supervision. Absolute control was abolished in 1882, which led to the expansion of theatrical activity, culminating in the founding of the Moscow Art Theatre in 1898.

The typical repertoire of the 1830s and 40s is succinctly characterised by Belinski:

> Plays which delight the bulk of the Aleksandrinsky Theatre audiences are divided into the poetic and the comic. The former are either translations of monstrous German dramas composed of sentimentalities, trivial effects and false situations, or homespun compositions in which inflated phraseology and soulless exclamations degrade time-honored historical names. Songs, dances, opportunely or inopportunely providing a favourite actress with a pretext for singing and dancing, as well as insanity scenes, are inevitable components of this kind of drama, which evokes clamors of delight and rages of applause. Comic pieces are invariably either translations of, or adaptations from French vaudevilles. These plays altogether stamped out both stagecraft and dramatic taste in the Russian theatre.[3]

It was in this climate and in these conditions that first Gogol and then Turgenev set about formulating a theory of drama and establishing a repertoire in keeping with the important role which they both felt the theatre had to play in their time.

Quite apart from providing an arena for the exercise of their creative talents, the theatre engaged the attentions of both Gogol and Turgenev for most of their lives, either

Theatrical Theories and Influences

as spectator, actor, critic or theorist. Gogol was attracted to the theatre while still at school. Although Turgenev was not so fine an actor, the art of acting appealed to him and he frequently took part in amateur theatrical performances. He read the works of Sumarokov and Fonvizin as a child and went to the theatre regularly from 1835 onwards. He was familiar with the work of Molière, Diderot and Lessing. He spent many hours at the theatre, especially during his stay in Paris in the 1840s, at a time when most of his own plays were written. His love for Shakespeare was life-long, and on the occasion of Shakespeare's 300th anniversary celebrations, in 1864, it was Turgenev who was called on to make the keynote speech. He learned Spanish so as to read Calderon, whose *Life is a Dream* he compared with *Hamlet* and whose *El Magico Prodigioso* he described as a Spanish *Faust*.

During the late 1850s the famous Potato Theatre on the Viardot country estate at Courtavenel opened its doors to a fee-paying public (admission was by potato), and Turgenev directed and acted in the plays of Racine and Molière in which Pauline Viardot also starred. Despite disappointments relating to the reception of his own dramatic work, his interest in the art of the theatre persisted and his enthusiasm was reawakened in later life by performances of his plays previously prevented by censorship, such as the famous 1879 revival of *A Month in the Country* with Marya Savina, when he was so impressed that he could scarcely credit himself with the authorship: 'Is it really I who wrote this?' he asked the young actress who had triumphed in the role of Verochka.[4]

In Paris during the 1830s, Gogol seldom missed an opera or theatre performance and was especially impressed by Molière. He was at the Théâtre Français for the 225th anniversary of Molière's birth, when he saw *Tartuffe* and *The Imaginary Invalid*. Despite his failure to become a professional actor, testimony as to Gogol's phenomenal acting talent is legion, drawn not only from accounts of his performances as a boy but, more often, from reminiscences of his readings from his own work given to groups of actors or to friends and fellow writers. Gogol also translated or adapted foreign dramas, the best-known example being an Italian comedy, *The Embarrassed Uncle* by Gio Giraud. However, his most important contribution to the Theatre of his day, apart from the plays, lies in the legacy of his theoretical writing.

Influential in the formation of Gogol's own critical outlook was the study he began, at the suggestion of Pushkin, of the history of dramatic criticism. While seeking to establish the originality of Russian drama, Gogol does not want to separate it from the rest of Europe and mentions in particular the importance, for the native tradition, of Molière, Lessing and Schiller. Between the years 1846–7, Gogol proposed a programme whereby the Russian spectator would be enabled to become familiar with the best products of the European drama. He attacked the tendencies which had led to the dominance in the theatre of superficial forms, inveighing against the genres of both vaudeville and melodrama as, in their separate ways, denying a living truth with their superabundance of horrors on the one hand and artificial invention of comic situations on the other. Gogol wanted a Russian theatre with an independent repertoire which presented plays concerned with national life:

> The position of Russian actors is pitiful. . . . What are they to do with these strange heroes, who are neither French nor German, but some sort of unbalanced people having absolutely no definite passion or

clear-cut physiognomy? . . . For God's sake, give us Russian characters, give us *our own selves*, our swindlers, our cranks! Onto the stage with them, for the people to laugh at![5]

For Gogol the theatre represented the means for the education of an entire nation. It is:

> . . . a rostrum from which a lively lesson is read to an entire crowd at once, where . . . a familiar but concealed vice is revealed and to the secret voice of general participation a familiar, timidly hiding, lofty emotion is exhibited . . .[6].

Gogol writes significantly about the function of laughter in the theatre. In *Conversation After The Play* he characterizes three different modes:

1. A light laughter which serves for the idle amusement and entertainment of people.
2. A laughter which is aroused by temporary irritation and a morbid, jaundiced disposition.
3. Laughter which issues wholly from man's bright nature, issues from it because at bottom there is an inexhaustible well which deepens everything, draws attention to what might have passed unnoticed and without whose penetrating force man would have been disheartened by life's trivialities and life's emptiness.[7]

Tracing the history of comic writing he asserts that, at first, comedy was a social and popular form as shown in the work of Aristophanes. Later, comedy entered the narrow path of the private and individual, of which the love intrigue was an essential part. He puts his own point of view in the words of the 'Second Lover of the Arts' in *Conversation After The Play*:

> The most important theme in the plot of a play is the desire to obtain a good position, to outshine and eclipse your rival by the brilliance of your wit, to avenge yourself for being disregarded or laughed at. Does not rank, money or a good marriage mean more to us today than love?[8]

The final sentence has been seen as programmatic of Gogol's drama as a whole, focusing on three main themes of his major plays: 'Rank', 'Marriage' and 'Money'.

He demanded that characters be constructed with a sense of their own inner life and that they be neither caricatures nor one-dimensional illustrations of a particular aspect of human behaviour. This had to be reflected in the acting. In his advice to actors given in the *Advance Notice To Those Wishing To Act The Government Inspector Properly*, Gogol emphasized the need not to exaggerate. The comedy arose from the complete seriousness with which each person is preoccupied with his or her own affairs. Only then would it become clear to the spectator precisely how trivial and banal these concerns are.

In Gogol's concept of the social function of the theatre, there is an anticipation of the theories of the Russian Symbolists, expressed at the turn of the twentieth century, to the effect that the theatre can exercise a religious function similar to that which existed in fifth-century Athens, in serving to reinforce a sense of social and spiritual cohesiveness. The Symbolist theorist, Vyacheslav Ivanov, proposed a new form of drama designed to recapture the religious quality of Greek tragedy, whose

Theatrical Theories and Influences

objective was 'to unite the crowd with the artist, whom inward necessity had separated from it, in a single combined celebration of worship.'[9]

The conditions which pertained in the theatre of Gogol's time can be seen to have been inimical to the realization of such a concept. A genuinely popular audience was not available, nor was the design of the proscenium arch stage sympathetically orientated towards the more open forms of a desirable 'theatre of communion', largely because of its structural tendency to emphasize the separation between the audience and that which is being enacted. Nevertheless, Gogol certainly saw the theatre as a potential focus of social unity as his remarks make clear:

> The theatre is by no means a trifle, nor a petty thing, if you take into consideration that it can accommodate a crowd of five or six thousand persons all at once, and that this multitude, whose members taken singly have nothing in common, can suddenly be shaken by the same shock, sob with the same tears, and laugh with the same general laughter. It is a kind of pulpit from which much good can be spoken to the world.[10]

Turgenev's attitude to the role and function of the theatre was equally serious and far-reaching. In the 1840s, especially, he shared with Gogol a strong desire to be a reformer of the Russian stage and a founder-creator of the new drama. One of the obstacles which lay in the path of this objective was the nature of the contemporary repertoire itself, especially the melodramatic, highminded, historico-pseudo-patriotic plays which were rife. Turgenev selected as his particular targets S. A. Gedeonov's *The Death of Lyapunov* and N V Kukolnik's *Commissioner-General Patkul*.

Nikolai Gogol and Ivan Turgenev

His article on Gedeonov, written in 1846, begins with some general remarks about the development of Russian dramaturgy. Although the drama has been imported from abroad, Turgenev feels that it has managed to put down deep roots in Russian soil and its appeal now extends to all ranks of society. Thanks to *The Government Inspector*, the Russian consciousness has undergone a change and a demand has developed for a drama which is true to life. Gogol 'has shown us the road down which our dramatic literature in time will go'.[11] The task of historical drama is not to recount facts but to present life as it actually existed in the past, to avoid the coldness of allegory as well as the tendency to lapse into the arid characteristics of chronicle form. Gedeonov's drama does not contain any errors of fact but is throughout imitative of its undistinguished predecessors. Whilst technically literate, its eclecticism 'does not serve to enrich the soul nor in one living warm word express a fresh view of Russia's past'.[12]

Turgenev is no less strict with Kukolnik's play. All the characters are very much like one another – turgid, sluggish and crude. Their dramatic language is impoverished and everything is sacrificed to the demands of declamation. The principal deficiency, however, lies in the absence of *narodnost* or popular feeling. Whilst leaning heavily on their western counterparts, dramatists like Kukolnik fail to emulate them in their most important respect – their ability to make themselves intelligible to the people. Both plays are seen as typical of the 'rhetorical school'. Neither possesses any living truth. Their 'hurrah-patriotic' nature, combined with their almost comical language is worthy of the latest French melodrama. Everything consists of declamation and falseness.[13]

Asserting a new direction in Russian theatre, Turgenev also feels forced to deal critically with the tradition represented by Schiller. (In this he was continuing the line adopted by Belinski.) Taking as his example *William Tell*, Turgenev emphasizes that the play has been composed to express a pre-determined philosophical point of view. While recognizing its merits, he objects to its 'worked-out' quality and inveighs against over-conscious creativity. At the same time he does not deny the very special qualities of Schiller's drama in which every character represents an aspect of human life and of the human spirit.[14]

In 1845, Turgenev turned his critical attention to Goethe's *Faust*. He describes it as a work of great historical significance but, even in this drama, he detects limitations stemming from Goethe's views which express a primitive stage in the awakening of human self-consciousness. The more mature standpoint, for Turgenev, is social rather than individual. At the same time, *Faust* appears alien to him from an artistic point of view as well. Part One of the tragedy serves as an apologia for human personality, a defence of the rights of a separate, suffering, isolated individual. This does not please Turgenev at all because for him the foundation stone of mankind is not man himself as a separable unit, but humanity, society, 'with its eternal, immemorial laws'.[15] He dislikes Part Two largely because it is presented in the form of an allegory, instead of realistically. For all its poetic greatness, *Faust* does not fully answer the spiritual demands of a new age in which concrete social problems have come to the fore, not just general philosophical ones.[16]

In the late 1840s and early 1850s, Turgenev was formulating his understanding of realism as the most fruitful method of artistic creation and, to this effect, supported the efforts of artists who seemed to him to be working in this direction. In the forefront, he cited the work of the young dramatist Alexander Ostrovski and highly praised his early play *It's a Family Affair*.

Turgenev had strong feelings about the kind of comedies which he wished to see performed on the Russian stage. His letters from France, in 1847, describe the pitiful state of the French theatre in the grip of Scribe. After seeing a play at the Palais Royale he wrote to Pauline Viardot:

> It was gay and I laughed a great deal . . . But, my God! how thin-blooded it all is, pale, faded and pitiful in comparison with what could be made of it by – I won't even mention Aristophanes – but say someone of his school! What wouldn't I give to be at a comedy which was fantastic, extravagant, funny and touching – pitiless towards everything weak and bad in society and even in man, causing him to laugh at his own poverty – raising us to the heights in order to laugh at that as well, singing the praises of stupidity in order to aggrandise it and throw it in the face of our pride. . . . What wouldn't I give for such a spectacle![17]

Both Turgenev and Gogol were concerned with the way plays should be staged. The year 1825 had seen the first mention in Russia of the term *regisseur*, meaning someone who was to have complete authority over every facet of production and free control of the cast. Also, between 1830 and 1850, stage scenery was beginning to become more representational. Turgenev was unique in his own time in the degree to which he embodied detailed stage directions within the playtext itself. He indicates very precisely the position of windows and doors etc, virtually supplying a complete plan of the stage. Gogol had provided detailed sketches of characters, costumes and set-

Theatrical Theories and Influences

tings for *The Government Inspector* and felt that matters of staging were so important that they should be left entirely to someone he called the 'actor–artist', without any official let or hindrance. He also suggested that part of the actor-artist's role was to take on all the secondary parts in a play, both for the benefit of the public and for the sake of the other actors who would have an ideal model to copy.[18]

Judged within the context of the theatre of their day, the views of both Gogol and Turgenev can be seen to have been well ahead of their time and were not susceptible to practical realization within the conditions prevailing in Nicolaevan Russia. As far as the requisite stage conditions are concerned, these were actually forthcoming with the founding, fifty years later, of the Moscow Art Theatre. As far as performance of their work is concerned, Gogol had to wait for the great twentieth-century interpretations of his drama by Meyerhold and others. Apart from occasional noteworthy productions of *A Month in the Country*, Turgenev may be said to be still awaiting the recognition which is his due as a dramatist and for interpretations of his plays which acknowledge their true value.

4
Gogol's Plays
1832—1842

It was in the wake of his first literary successes, in 1832, that Gogol turned his attention to the writing of plays. He began work, late in the year, on two comedies – *The Order Of Vladimir, Third Class* and *The Suitors*. Because of fears of censorship and because of problems involved in writing this, his first play, *The Order Of Vladimir* was abandoned and all that remains are four fragments. The second play went through many versions before appearing, in 1842, as *Marriage*.

Gogol spoke of his plans for *The Order of Vladimir, Third Class* in a letter written in February 1833, when he described it as full of 'malice, salt and laughter'.[1] The plot was to have concerned the passionate desire of a Petersburg official, called variously Barsukov (Badger) and Burdyukov (Wineskin), to be awarded the medal of the Order of St Vladimir. The play was to have culminated in the thwarting of Barsukov's ambitions, as a result of which he went mad and imagined himself to actually be the Vladimir medal. The theme of madness and alienation,

Gogol's Plays 1832-1842

here to have been treated comically, became the more serious subject of *Diary of a Madman*. The thwarting of Ivan Petrovich Barsukov is planned by his friend, Alexander Ivanovich Prolyotov, and Barsukov's brother, Khristofor Petrovich Burdyukov, a provincial landowner, who declares that Barsukov has swindled him of their aunt's legacy. Burdyukov seeks Prolyotov's help in bringing a lawsuit against his brother. A second sub-plot deals with the affairs of Barsukov's widowed sister, Marya Alexandrovna, who connives with one Sobachkin, whom she secretly despises, to effect a breach between her son, Misha, and the girl he wishes to marry. Yet another sub-plot was to have involved the servants on Barsukov's staff who are organizing a servants' ball for the better class of lackey. Each 'fragment' is a self-contained playlet but without any clear links between the four. They are significant in so far as the treatment of their dramatic themes anticipates the later, more important, comedies.

The first fragment, or short play, *Morning of a Man of Affairs*, was published in the journal *The Contemporary* under Pushkin's editorship, in 1836, with the sub-title *Petersburg Scenes*. It is set in an office, which is also part of Barsukov's home, and begins with a familiar Gogolian motif of repetitions. A bell is rung, three times, before a lackey appears – his excuse being his 'affairs' (which happen to be 'cleaning boots'), an ironic contrast with the 'affairs' of Barsukov referred to in the play's title. The official's first command is to order his dog to be brought, which he proceeds to address repetitiously with banal terms of endearment while tying a piece of paper, in the shape of a ribbon, to its tail. There then follows a conversation between Barsukov and his friend Prolyotov about a card game, touching with portentous and absurd solemnity on the themes of 'Time' (how a person of consequence can tell when it is six o'clock) and chamois leather vests – a typically Gogolian piece of comic juxtaposition. They then pass to the subject of a highly-placed dignitary, from whom Barsukov hopes for advancement, and whose ear Prolyotov appears to have. Barsukov is on tenterhooks to learn whether the high official approves of him, whereupon Gogol indulges his comic taste for apparent non-sequiturs by having Prolyotov studiously cast his eyes aloft and comment, evasively, on the pseudo-baroque ceiling decoration in terms which draw our attention to its pretentious vulgarity.

The following scene between a clerk and the two officials serves to underline the techniques of Barsukov's bureaucratic management. This is conveyed by the circuitous manner in which he issues orders, so that the final decision, and hence the responsibility, is contrived to devolve on someone other than himself. The theme of petty bureaucracy combined with obsessional orderliness is emphasized when Barsukov points out to the clerk that the margins of some papers brought for signature are not straight and that, as these are due to go before the Head of Department, he could be arrested for negligence. Barsukov recalls the disorder which reigned in the department before his arrival: 'It was a regular Tower of Babel! There must be order, order in everything!' The grounds for his lapse into insanity are established at the outset.

The Lawsuit, the second fragment, concerns a meeting between Prolyotov and Burdyukov at the conclusion of which the former agrees to act as legal representative in bringing charges against Barsukov. It was first published in 1842 and, of all the fragments, is unique in having been performed during Gogol's lifetime. The scene, once again, is a departmental office. The play again begins with a pattern of repetitions but here it is a series of belches emitted by Prolyotov, who begins to assume the proportions of a mediaeval figure of Gluttony, indicated by a typically Gogolian play on words: ... *k chortu, i v chetvyorty!* (It's the fourth one. To the devil with it!) where the words *chetvyorty* (fourth) and *chort* (devil) become linked. This is one of many references to the devil in Gogol's drama and illustrates as well his tendency to exploit pun and double-meaning.

A lackey announces the arrival of Burdyukov, who explains his intention of bringing his brother, Barsukov, to justice. The importance of the notion of community in Gogol's ideology has been indicated. Central to the idea of community is the family unit. The fact that, in this instance, brother is up in arms against brother is symptomatic of a deep-rooted social malaise. The brother's vindictiveness, which is a source of satisfaction to Prolyotov, serves to intensify the irony. The characters in the play begin to take on the shapes of a menagerie. The brother is referred to by Burdyukov as 'a beast'. He himself is called a 'country bear'. The deceased aunt's name, Zherebtsova, is similar to the Russian word for 'foal'.

The terms of the will which Barsukov is supposed to have falsified are highly ironic. The litigious brother has, humiliatingly, been left 'three woolly petticoats and all the implements in the storehouse as well as two feather-beds, a china service, sheets, nightcaps and the devil only knows what rags besides!' A flaw in the will's legality is discovered when Burdyukov points to the apparently false signature. Prolyotov sees this as a heaven-sent opportunity to contest the will and undo his enemy, as well as proof positive of Barsukov's being 'a swine and a cheat'. His joy knows no bounds as he contemplates a sequence of events which will culminate in Barsukov's downfall.

The action of the third fragment, *The Servants' Hall*, takes place in the house of an important official, referred to as the *barin* (master). In the original version the *barin* was meant to have been Barsukov and the action set, presumably, at a time following his promotion. The play begins with the familiar pattern of repetitions. At the rise of the curtain, three servants are discovered sleeping in identical positions with their heads resting on each others' shoulders. In Beckettian fashion they are brought to life simultaneously by a loud bell. The first scene consists of a discussion between the three servants and an 'alien lackey', Andryushka, which centres around the question of the division of labour among servants. The contrast becomes one between 'insiders' and 'outsiders', but where the so-called 'alien lackey', in belonging to an older order, emerges as the least 'alienated'. In the house of the rich master there is strict division between functions. It is pointed out by Grigory, one of the servants, that 'lackeys' do not 'work'; for that purpose there are 'workmen'. Beneath the humour Gogol is making a serious if nostalgic point that, under the old dispensation, there was no division of labour and field serfs could double as house-serfs and perform several functions. The new process, which differentiates strictly between individual functions, strikes at the integral fabric of society and perpetuates the process of mechanical division which produces fragmentation.

In a brief scene which follows, we are treated to a view of the schizophrenic side of servant life as Grigory, in quick succession, humiliates a casual caller, grabs at the skirts of a housemaid in a grotesque attempt at flirtation, snaps to attention whilst solemnly adjusting his countenance as he might his dress, then lapses into vacancy while studiously picking his nose.

Gogol's Plays 1832-1842

The final section of the fragment might be sub-titled 'What happens to authority when the master is away'. Into the power vacuum steps the senior lackey, Lavrenti. There ensues a conversation between him and a visiting servant girl, Anna Gavrilovna. They provide, in parodied form, an impersonation of the refined manners of their superiors – standards by which they themselves are enslaved. At the same time, a sense of an undercurrent of primitive urges is suggested, past the preciousness of the language, which hints that Lavrenti and 'Annushka' are sitting on thorns until they are together in private. The conversation concerns a subscription ball to be held by the servants. The theme of the division of labour is extended and becomes associated with a corresponding alienation from natural functions, from dirt and from manual work. Annushka is concerned that the coachman should not be invited to the ball because he smells. Lavrenti, in a paroxysm of delicacy, refers to the fact that a coachman's duties are, after all, associated, so to speak, with 'ordure'. In so doing he manages to impress Annushka with both his articulacy and his sense of refinement. The underlying lust is glossed over by the formal niceties of language and Gogol stresses the incongruity of having Lavrenti explain the inarticulacy and lack of refinement of others as being a product of 'nature'. This is followed by an invitation to enter his room.

Scenes from High Society, the final fragment, belongs like *The Servants' Hall* to the years 1839–40. The scene is set in the house of an elderly society lady, Marya Alexandrovna, whose thirty-year-old bachelor son, Misha, she still controls and treats like a schoolboy, much to his chagrin. Her domination of him is only exceeded by the tyranny which socially prescribed norms exercize over her. The mother is concerned that her son quit the civil service and don the uniform of an officer, because she has overheard a Princess Alexandrina pour scorn on civilians. Misha is a mere instrument of her social vendetta and he complains that he would simply look ridiculous in uniform on account of his plumpness. Secondly, the mother announces, she wants to marry him off to Princess Shlepokhvostova (Draggletail), who may be foolish and absent-minded but at least has the virtue of being mild-tempered. When Misha objects and suggests that marriage should be an affair of the heart, his mother accuses him of being a Liberal with radical ideas, which she attributes to the influence of one Sobachkin.

It emerges that Misha wishes to marry the daughter of a certain Odosimov, whom the mother suggests is a drunkard, whose daughter is a mere gold-digger, his wife a cook and their relations either policemen or potboys. Her sabotaging tactic is to stage a fainting fit. Emotional blackmail is clearly a familiar strategy and there is a serious psychological strain beneath the vaudeville surface. The fact that, during her attack of hysteria, she addresses her son as 'Mashka' (the diminutive of a girl's name) is an aspect of the control which she exercises over him. Ambiguity of sexual role, or a confusion of male and female characteristics, are frequent elements in Gogol's work.

The rest of the playlet consists of an extended scene between Marya Alexandrovna and Sobachkin, whom she hopes to use in thwarting the proposed match between Misha and the Odosimov girl. Sobachkin emerges as a thoroughly unscrupulous character, a slanderer and a coward, as well as a complacently self-centred narcissist. Marya Alexandrovna's instinctive contempt for him as a social inferior gives way to her interest in his scandal-mongering and her need to use him in her strategy. She exploits Sobachkin by pointing out his attractiveness to women. Sobachkin offers to seduce and compromise the Odosimov girl and when Marya Alexandrovna sheds doubt on his powers as a gigolo, he declares he will cut off his head and present it to her in the event of failure. Marya Alexandrovna has already been presented to us as a form of castrator in her relationship with her son; here, Sobachkin casts her in the role of a Salomé or a Judith.

Sobachkin seizes the opportunity to extract a 'loan' of 2000 roubles and, left alone on stage, embarks on a long, superbly self-revealing soliloquy, which concludes the fragment. Our final view of him anticipates a moment in *Dead Souls* when, in a manner reminiscent of Chichikov, Gogol has him contemplate his image in a mirror, while ruminating aloud on how best to grow his side-whiskers.

Alfred

Gogol's attraction to large-scale historical subjects has already been mentioned, as has his plan for multi-volume histories of the Middle Ages and the Ukraine. However, apart from the occasional essay published in *Arabesques*, the fictional *Taras Bulba*, and the sketched outline of a drama based on Ukrainian history entitled *The Shaved-Off Moustache*, only one other historical work remains extant from Gogol's pen – the truncated version of a full-length historical drama based on the life and times of the Anglo-Saxon king, Alfred the Great.

The main historical source for this drama would appear to have been a French translation of Hallam's *Europe in the Middle Ages*, which Gogol had drawn on for his university lectures. The action of the play takes place in a ninth-century England which has been overrun by the Danes following the death of Alfred's brother. At the opening a crowd of 'thanes' and 'churls' are waiting by the seashore for the arrival of the new king, Alfred, who has been away receiving his training in Papal Rome. The first scene informs us that the people are facing problems, both from the marauding Danes and also from their own 'thanes', who rob them of their land and press them into service. 'Nobody, according to Anglo-Saxon law, can insult or enslave a free man', says one of the characters, Kudred. Another, Egbert, himself a thane, states the terms of an ideal equality: 'Although thou art a churl and I a thane, yet, because thou art an Anglo-Saxon and an honest man, I shake thy hand'.

The opening scene also describes in idealized terms, the French court and Papal Rome, with its majestic ceremonies, its cloth-of-gold, crimson mantles and stately processions. By contrast, the Danes are described as sea-monsters and agents of the devil. In this fashion, the central conflict enshrined within the play is revealed to be between the spirits of Paganism and Christianity. Hubbo, king of the Danes, prays to the spirit of Odin for support. Alfred, supported by his Roman education in the Catholic faith, summons the spiritual help of Christ and the Virgin Mary, as well as calling on the nationalistic ghost of St George.

In Act I, the patient wait of the watchers on the shore is rewarded, after one false alarm, by the arrival of King Alfred who no sooner disembarks than he departs for York, leaving a group of thanes behind to debate his merits as a monarch. They are interrupted by the arrival by sea of King Hubbo, who states the violent terms of a faith based on the might of arms, belief in Odin, and unadulterated male heroism. This runs, uninterrupted, into a short scene between Alfred and his followers, which is interesting for the expression it gives of Alfred's ideology. It emerges that his notion of the ideal nation state is a model based on the Roman Empire, but christianized. In this respect, it is clear that Alfred sees himself as a resurrected Constantine. News is brought of the sacking of London by the Danes and Alfred sets off to do battle. The scene concludes with a celebration of Alfred's virtues as a bold and intelligent monarch.

It is clear from the beginning of the subsequent scene that Alfred's forces have been beaten. He rallies them by appealing to their faith in the power of the Christian forces which support their cause. Hubbo's pursuing army enters and a short battle ensues, which, this time, leaves Alfred the victor. In victory he is magnanimous and spares Hubbo, causing him to swear on his oath to leave England's shores and never to raid the country again. Hubbo does so, but confides in his comrades that the oath will be broken and that they will live to fight another day. At this point the manuscript breaks off. Reconstructions of Gogol's intentions suggest that what was to follow included the return of Hubbo and the defeat of Alfred, who retreats into exile. There was then to have been an episode in the forests of Somerset, where Alfred gathers an army of peasant partisans (this section was to have included the famous burning of the cakes). Presumably, the play would have ended with the routing of the Danes and the crowning of Alfred.[2]

The nineteenth-century critic, Chernyshevski, felt that Gogol was trying to trace an analogy between King Alfred and Peter the Great. In the absence of an ideal monarch, Alfred appeared to approximate to the historical figures of the then popular historico-patriotic drama. Another important theme which Chernyshevski pointed to was the depiction of the internecine strife and petty intriguing between members of the English nobility, who persecuted their own people instead of turning their attention to the enemy. Gogol later returned to the subject of mythological heroism in the Ukrainian 'historical fable', *Taras Bulba*.

Gamblers

Gamblers must be one of the greatest comedies never to have found a place in the world repertoire. The play never seems to have been popular even in Russia, where *Marriage* and *The Government Inspector* are pillars of the repertory. *Marriage* is perhaps a difficult play for English-speaking audiences and, despite the availability of good translations, has rarely been performed. *Gamblers*, by comparison, is an apparently straightforward one-act play with a directly comprehensible appeal to a non-Russian audience, and Constance Garnett's translation has been available since 1926. What can be the reason for this neglect? The only possible explanation is that the true quality of the play has never been appreciated. Gogol may, in part, be held responsible for this. He worked on it intermittently between 1836 and its publication in 1842, when he included it among the 'Dramatic Fragments And Other Scenes' rather than with the two major plays. It was also Gogol himself who stated that *Gamblers* should not be termed a 'comedy' but merely 'comic scenes'. Its first performance was given in Moscow, in February 1843, with Shchepkin in the role of Uteshitelny, as a curtain-raiser to *Marriage*. Neither was a success. However, the literary critic N. A. Kotlyarevski described *Gamblers* as 'one of the most perfect dramatic works from the standpoint of technique'.[3]

The world of *Gamblers* is a bewildering hall of mirrors, where one reality gives way to another in an ever-receding perspective until, finally, everything disappears

Gogol's Plays 1832-1842

and we are left with nothing. The plot is both simple and extremely complicated. Ikharev, a cardsharp, plans independently to swindle three fellow-travellers at an inn. His plot is discovered and he enters into a scheme with the three he intended swindling to fool a third party who, unbeknown to Ikharev, is a colleague of the others. Also in the plot to swindle Ikharev are two more masquerading under assumed names, one of whom, although he believes himself to be part of the plot, is also an unwitting victim of it. Both Ikharev and he are left at the end of the play, the one dispossessed of 80,000 roubles, the other of 3,000 and the conspirators have vanished like a mirage. We are left, like Ikharev and the fictitiously named Glov, rubbing our eyes in disbelief and wondering whether what we have seen actually happened.

The point of the play is not the surprise at the end when we realize at the same time as Ikharev that he has been the victim of an elaborately staged game. The point is the game itself, and this can only be appreciated if the audience is fully aware in advance of all the ironic elements in the plot. It is the fable which is important and, in this sense, the play is a model of classicism which bears comparison with *Oedipus Rex*. There, the full resources and full effect of the dramatic irony are intrinsically dependent on close familiarity with the outcome. The tragic *frisson* derived from individual moments of the plot is thus deepened. The comic density of *Gamblers* is likewise intensified when each moment takes on its full weight of implication derived from foreknowledge of and familiarity with the events in the drama.

The play is both a moral tract about the meaning of life and a brilliant Jonsonian parable of life as theatre, or play, with a gallery of Jonsonian types who might have stepped straight out of the pages of *Volpone* or *The Alchemist*. It can even be described as 'Brechtian' in the way it treats gambling as an analogy for specific economic forms of life based on the rapid accumulation of capital through speculation. The play's epigraph – 'Deeds Of Days Long Past' – should alert us to the fact that, in Aesopian fashion, our attention is being directed to matters with an especially contemporary relevance.

At the beginning, the 'hero', Ikharev, and his servant, Gavryushka, are being shown to their room at an inn in the town they have just reached. The inn servant points to the bed, *pokoychik*, and says it is a very quiet room, *pokoyny*, with no noise whatsoever. Gogol emphasizes this through repetitions of the word, an old fashioned form of *spokoyny* (quiet) but, in its old form, a pun on 'the late', or 'deceased'. What the servant is saying amounts to:

> It's 'dead' here. There's no noise. All the numbers are full.

where the 'numbers' *(nomera* in Russian) refer to both the rooms and the numbers on their sealed doors. The fleas and bedbugs which the servant refers to are correspondingly metamorphosed into the worms which feed off the living-dead flesh of the inhabitants. We are at an inn but, at the same time, we are in a house of the dead, among the living dead. A direct connection is established between the living corpses of the action and their speculative enterprise when Ikharev refers, at the end of Scene 13, to a waste of life while ostensibly referring to frozen assets:

> And how much of it is wasted without being put into circulation! How many dead fortunes there are which lie like corpses in the banks!

Gogol's Plays 1832-1842

The play has mediaeval dimensions, developing like a sermon on hell and damnation preached from the pulpit which is the theatre of Gogol's own mind. The perspectives extend from the cradle to the grave and from heaven to hell. This is hell because the inhabitants have lost sight of heaven. Like Ikharev, they work in darkness, perfecting their game of hazard which is a substitute for a philosophy of life. The truth, admittedly, can only be glimpsed through a glass, darkly, Reality, or truth, lies 'on the other side'. But the search for this 'truth' is hideously parodied in the deciphering of what is written on the face of the cards by minutely attentive study of their reverse pattern. Central to this mode of procedure is the obsession with numbers and figures and statistical accumulation, accompanied by the total neglect of the larger world of moral and spiritual absolutes. The result is a world of liars and cheats where human potential is squandered in the interests of accumulating trash. Everything becomes reduced to the mechanistic terms and language of the stock exchange. Even the concept of 'play' is reduced. For Gogol, at its highest, acting and play are aspects of the theatre as temple. Here the notions are reduced to deceit, hazard and falseness. *Gamblers* is about 'play', both as card-game and as theatre, but here the disguise is donned merely to deceive, to gain an advantage and to reduce to confusion – not to elevate, enlighten and ennoble. The world has always been a stage, but here it has become the haunt of frauds and mountebanks.

Gogol is at pains to point out that this is a man-made world. This fact is stressed by the total absence of women, except in surrogate form. As Eric Bentley has said, apropos of *Gamblers*:

> The culture *as a whole* [his italics] is anti- feminine in

its bias, in its feelings, which is only another way of saying that what we have got – what we have had for many centuries – is male supremacy, a fact of rule, of domination, which spreads out into a million facts of mores and psychology.[4]

Ikharev appears sexually abnormal. Gambling, an all-male preoccupation, cheating and swindling, are referred to as 'passions'; they are substitute occupations. Ikharev even has a surrogate sexual relationship with his favourite pack of cards, which he names Adelaida Ivanovna. 'She'd make a good wife for you', Uteshitelny jokes with one of the gang, Krugel. The point about 'all-maleness' is brought home with comic force, in Scene 16, when the fraudulent young Glov has been introduced to the unsuspecting Ikharev by the rest of the gang:

Uteshitelny: Wait, my boy, let me embrace you!
Shvokhnev: Let me embrace him too. (*embraces him*).
Ikharev: Permit me to embrace him. (*embraces him*).
Krugel: Well if that's the way it is, I'll embrace him too! (*embraces him*)

At this juncture the servant, Alexey, enters carrying a bottle of champagne, 'holding the cork in with his finger, which then bursts and flies to the ceiling. . . .' The symbolism is inescapable. Much has been written about Gogol's supposed homosexuality. What could be a more witty comment at the expense of his interpreters than this visual joke levelled at an all-male 'togetherness' with its sexual undertones? The only 'real' woman in the play is Glov's sister whom, he suggests, he would like to 'have a go at' himself if she were not his sister. But is she real? She may be as fictitious as his name turns out to be. Under these conditions, names mean nothing and that which seems most real turns out to be most insubstantial.

The world of *Gamblers* is composed of bits and pieces. Ikharev's estates are scattered here and there. His retinue of servants is described by Gavryushka as rigidly divided according to the laws of the division of labour. The notion of true collectivity is travestied in the form of a cartel of cheats, none of whom trusts the other. Nothing that anyone says is meaningful; the talk of social unity and honesty is mere farce. Even the expression of righteous anger is part of the act. The most sacred sentiments, in Gogol's terms, become as nothing in their mouths. The world is like a balloon which goes 'bust' when your cards add up to more than 21. Everything is light as air and hollow at the centre, while he who holds the bank, or 'mounts a bank', is king. The mystic runes of existence are to be read on the backs of cards. The 'higher secrets' relate to an education in cheating. There is the typical Gogolian emphasis on youth and its perversion. Ikharev, like Chichikov, has been trained from his youth in the values of this society. There is even a parody on the birth of Christ, in Scene 8, where Shvokhnev (whose name cannot be pronounced without phlegm collecting in the mouth preparatory to spitting) tells of Ivan Mikhailovich Kuibyshev, whom God rewarded with an extraordinary son of whose powers remarkable rumours were heard, so that learned people flocked from all corners of the land to question him and hear his answers. His 'gifts', or his 'art', turns out to be a phenomenal talent for palming cards while shuffling them. 'The key to the pattern is on the reverse side', declares Uteshitelny – a sentiment with which Gogol might, ironically, be said to agree.

Nikolai Gogol and Ivan Turgenev

In the same scene Uteshitelny (his name means 'consoler'), gives a lesson on the division of labour. The talk is of someone who earns 5000 roubles a year for marking cards. 'It's a very important duty', says Ikharev. 'It's bound to be like that', replies Uteshitelny:

> It's what is called in political economy the division of labour. Take a carriage-builder – he does not build the whole of the carriage himself: he hands the job partly to the blacksmith, partly to the upholsterer. Human life wouldn't be long enough otherwise.

The intellectual ironies of what it means to be 'human' are throughout of this order, on a par with the ironies of the plot. A central, classical irony relates to the role of Ikharev himself. Early in the play he describes the way in which the spots on the backs of the cards dazzle him. In Scene 8, he describes the manner in which he learned his art, slaving away in darkness, out of the light of the sun. His doctor feared inflammation of the eyes. He appears to suffer from Galileo's complaint derived from the observation of sunspots but, instead of gazing upwards he has been gazing downwards in artificial light. Gogol has reversed the myth of Icarus (*Ikar* in Russian – hence Ikharev) whose servant we note is called Gabriel (Gavrila). These would-be angels no longer aspire towards the light and there is little danger of their flying too near the sun. The world of heaven is remote and we are among the devils in hell.

The devil's name is invoked on no fewer than thirty-five occasions during the course of this one-act play, and with increasing frequency whenever cards are being played. When Uteshitelny and his cronies vanish with Ikharev's money they say they are expected in 'Nizhny' which, while referring to the town of Nizhny Novgorord, also suggests 'down there' (*nizhny* = lower). 'Down there' is 'a market', where the gang intend to continue their sharp practices in the social equivalent of the infernal regions.

During the course of the play life is described as 'boredom to death', as a 'fatal interval', and there is a realization that this 'is nothing to joke about'. In face of this recognition there is a sense of 'To hell with everything! *Va banque!*', as the young Glov shouts, repeatedly, while being tossed in the air by the gang to the accompaniment of the refrain 'In you we see a father . . .'. The sentiment is echoed in the smashing of glasses against heels into a thousand fragments. 'I'll leave my money to my son as an inheritance', says the (apparently childless) Ikharev. That which is being gambled away and left to chance is the very future itself, as these living-dead fritter away existence, conscious of the moment only. What do people mean anyway? What does it matter if *Psoi Stakhich* is, in actual fact, *Fenteflei Perpentich?* Both are equally absurd and, in this cynical world, 'What the hell does it matter?' 'I am as much Glov as you are the Emperor of China', says Glov junior to Ikharev when the masks are off. The implication is that they might just as well be numbers in their coffin-like rooms; there is little that is intrinsically 'human' about them. If there is anything in a name, 'the devil can take it'. Ikharev's condition at the end of the play is described as close to madness. To imagine oneself to be the Emperor of China is, simultaneously, as real and as arbitrary as everything else seems to be in a world of this order; but that fate was reserved for Poprishchin in *Diary of a Madman*.

Marriage

The plot of *Marriage*, subtitled 'An absolutely incredible incident in two acts', concerns the attempts, aided and abetted by two matchmakers – one amateur, the other professional – to marry the dilatory bachelor, Podkolyosin, to the merchant's daughter, Agafya Tikhonovna, in which he finds himself in competition with four other suitors. He is cajoled and badgered to the point of success by the amateur matchmaker, his friend Kochkaryov, but when finally faced with the prospect of wedded bliss, Podkolyosin escapes by leaping from a first floor window.

The first variant of the play belongs to the year 1833. At this stage it was called both *The Suitors* and *The Provincial Suitor* and was set in the country rather than in the St Petersburg of the final version, now retitled *Marriage*, which was completed in 1841 and first published the following year. The play's first production was in St Petersburg, on 9 December 1842, and this was closely followed by a Moscow production on 5 February 1843. I. I. Sosnitski, who acted in it, felt that the play lacked comedy and that there was no motivation for the characters:

God knows why people arrive and why they leave.[5]

Belinski, who was at the first performance, described it as being hissed off the stage, it was so vilely acted. The reactionary Bulgarin, writing in *The Northern Bee*, in 1842, said that *Marriage* had about as much right to the name of comedy as *Dead Souls* had to be called a poem. It had 'no plot, no denouement, no characters, no wit and not even any joy'.[6]

The problems which Gogol experienced with the censor

over *Marriage* were of a petty and irritating order. The main insistence was that anything which could be construed as casting a slight on Russian values and institutions be eliminated. For example, a reference to 'the seamstress, the one who used to live with the Senate senior-secretary' was excized by the censor, as was Zhevakin's reference to the strange names of his comrades in the squadron, because these were considered a slur on baptismal rites. There were many other cuts of a similar nature now all, fortunately, restored.

Reactions to the play in print have varied, with some critics placing it on the same artistic level as *The Government Inspector* and *Dead Souls*. Others find the play far too contrived and implausible, pointing to the fact that under Russian law you cannot have a marriage on the same day as the engagement and the idea of Zhevakin's seventeenth rejection being too ludicrous. Critics have either described the play as pure farce or have seen something deeper in Podkolyosin's vacillation, which makes of him 'a travestied and trivialized Hamlet'.[7] Others have detected something symbolic in the texture of the play as a whole, with a faint suggestion of mysterious forces at work.[8] Dostoevski singled out *Marriage* as a particularly enigmatic work, needing further deciphering to be properly appreciated.[9] Recent Soviet criticism has had some interesting insights, although there is a tendency to see the play very much as a realistic depiction of the manners and mores of the merchant class and civil servants of the period. Inna Vishnevskaya is unique in acknowledging the importance of the world of Gogol's folk-tales to an understanding of the play, and even acknowledges the presence of the devil.[10]

There have been interesting, but no outstanding, productions of the play in Russia and very few in English-speaking countries. *Marriage* has, however, had an enormous influence on later Russian drama. The depiction of the bureaucracy was taken up by Sukhovo-Kobylin in his trilogy and by Saltykov-Shchedrin, but the most influenced of all was Ostrovski, whose *A Lucrative Post*, as well as the complete Balzaminov trilogy, owes a strong debt to *Marriage*, as do a whole range of his character types, including merchants' wives and marriage brokers. *Marriage* was also one of Chekhov's favourite plays.

Marriage developed to an extraordinary degree in the ten years during which Gogol worked on it. The basic plot throughout remained the same but the thematic material was broadened and deepened. One of the most important innovations lay in Gogol's decision to double the central characters and provide a counterpart for Agafya in Podkolyosin and to double the number of matchmakers. It is this notion of 'doubleness' or 'duality' which Gogol, piece by piece, integrated into the fabric of his original comedy so that the play came to be about 'couples' rather than about a group of suitors. Marriage is about bringing two sides together; matchmaking is a similar process – a destruction of singleness, or singularity, and the introduction of 'doubleness'. No doubt this was one of the aspects of the play which appealed to Dostoevski, whose own *The Double* was published in 1846.

Podkolyosin is 'under the wheel' as his name implies. Its origin appears to derive from a line in the first version of the play: 'A wife without a husband – is like a cart without a wheel'. Podkolyosin is now under (*pod*) the wheel (*koleso*). This poor man's Agamemnon has taken upon himself the harness of necessity; but here, the pattern of necessity, a tragic concept, has lost all its dignity and has become reduced to a question of habit. To be 'under the wheel' is to be a victim of repetitious routine and subject

Gogol's Plays 1832-1842

to an essential sameness. At the same time, the ultimate end of human aspiration, the concept of destiny itself, has found its apotheosis in 'marriage'. Gogol weighs the trivial in the scales of the great and balances the ideal against the real, rendering the minor version of each comical in the process. What marriage actually symbolizes, for Gogol, would appear to be something profound. It implies the integration of two halves of reality; the recognition of the fundamental duality which underlines all phenomena and an attempt to bring these into harmonious relationship. But for a marriage to mean something, on a physical or abstract level, there must be something there to bring together, otherwise you have the coming together of nothing. At the centre of the play there lies this nullity, nonexistence, a yawning void.

The drama opens with Podkolyosin lying on his divan ruminating. The room is described as that of a bachelor. The word is far stronger in Russian than in English. *Kholostyak* means more than a man who is unmarried, it carries powerful overtones of nothingness, blankness (one of its meanings is, in fact, a 'blank cartridge'). He is philosophizing in fairly aimless fashion, the general drift of his argument being that when you are on your own and you begin to think about things you realize that life is a vale of tears and that, in the end, we all have to ... MARRY??!! It is as if the focus is comically reduced. Infinity is reduced to the finite and particular but the destination of the argument is illogical and arbitrary. The purpose of life has become 'to get married'. Marriage has actually become symptomatic of the evasion of a purpose in life. At the same time it stands for everything which is *being* evaded, hence its terrors. It is potentially both everything and nothing. Through its finiteness one gains a peek into infinity. Through its fake doubleness there is yet a glimpse of the duality which implies other realities, genuine complexity, the sub-conscious, other worlds. But what has marriage actually become? Instead of the mystery, it is just another mode of consumption. In *The Suitors*, the servant was sent to find suitors at the market and talked of returning with *shest shtuk* (six pieces). She might just as well have been talking of candles or saucepans. Similarly, marriage for most of the suitors in the play involves entering into a commodity relationship, or a sexual relationship in which the wife is still an object.

In his opening speech Podkolyosin makes us aware of the relationship between marriage and another type of consumption. He talks of having missed *myasoyed* – a week of the church calendar when marriages can be solemnized, as the church forbids this during weeks of fast. So marriage is associated with meat-eating (*myaso* = meat). One of the suitors is called Zhevakin (*zhevat'* = to chew). Yaichnitsa (scrambled egg) says he wants a wife with some meat on her. It is a world in which expressionist motifs coexist with a comic-realist surface.

The opening conversation between Podkolyosin and his servant Stepan is a remarkable anticipation of the spiritual nature of the discourse between Hamm and Clov in Beckett's *Endgame*. It is centred around repetitions and negations and the general effect is one of circularity and nullity. 'Is the tailor sewing my dress coat?' asks Podkolyosin. 'Yes', answers Stepan, 'he's already begun to sew the buttonholes'. At first sight this looks like completion, but it also suggests the beginning. The tailor has begun with the holes first. He is sewing the hole at the centre of the play. The word for the hole which the tailor is sewing is *petlya*, which has the alternative meaning of 'noose'. He is making both a buttonhole and something associated with capital punishment. 'Is he making dress coats for anybody else?' asks Podkolyosin. 'Yes' answers Stepan, 'he has a good number of dress coats hanging'. Suddenly, the image is of rows of ex-bachelors, in their black frock coats, hanging from a gallows. The phrase *pod venets*, as a metaphor for marriage, is used on four occasions in the play, meaning 'under the wreath, or chaplet' (to stand *pod venets* meaning to 'be at the altar'). The final occasion when the phrase is used occurs during Podkolyosin's speech before leaping out of the window: '. . . in a moment I'll be *pod venets*; there's no leaving now – the *karyeta* (cart or carriage) is there already, and everything stands in readiness.' The image becomes that of the condemned man on the cart, beneath the noose, waiting for the drop. As the Fool puns in *Twelfth Night*: 'Many a good hanging prevents a bad marriage . . .'. In Gogol's world, marriage, sex and death are interwoven. A leap in the dark, into the unknown, can only be shown, in parodied form, as a leap out of the window.

In Gogolian fashion, the play also deals in mirror images. 'Don't blame the mirror if your mug is crooked', as the epigraph to *The Government Inspector* runs. The characters look into mirrors for desirable reflections and see only what they wish to see. The one exception is Podkolyosin, who does not like what he sees in the mirror – a *memento mori* in the shape of a grey hair. When he smashes the mirror, Kochkaryov offers to get him another, which Podkolyosin refuses because it would be a cheap distorting one (it would not come from 'The English shop'). The play which Gogol gives us is the one seen through the distorting reflection of the cheap mirror. It is a dual aspect of the truth which the characters fail to recognize. They are grotesques, described by each other as 'beasts', 'witches', 'monsters', 'swine'. Names of endearment are 'cockroach' and 'pigsnout'. Characters' names are 'Dishwater' and 'Stewed-Too-Long'. The world is composed of distorted images. Zhevakin tells the comic-horrific tale of his crippled name-sake, whose knee tendon has been threaded by a bullet, so that when you stood next to him, his knee kept hitting you in the back. As in the world of Samuel Beckett, mobility is a problem. Podkolyosin has difficulty in getting off his sofa. Yaichnitsa is so gross he can hardly get through the door. Onuchkin's legs are so thin they can scarcely support his weight. The state of crippledom appears to pass over into inanimate objects. The foundations of Agafya's house are described as half wood (rotten) and half stone. The one will undermine the other in both the animate and inanimate worlds of the play.

In the mirror-images, the characters metamorphose before our eyes. Kochkaryov creeps up behind Podkolyosin, who is examining himself in the mirror, so absorbed with his own reflection that his sudden realization of Kochkaryov's presence startles him like a ghost. At the same time there is the suggestion that Kochkaryov's reflection did not appear in the mirror and, indeed, there is something of the devil about him. (In an early draft of the play he was called Kokhtin which derives from *Kogti* = claws or nails.) One of his roles is as tempter. He baits the trap of marriage with women's hands: '. . . and suddenly the sweet little woman sits down beside you and with her little hand she . . .'. Kochkaryov wishes his own married state on Podkolyosin and there is a distinct suggestion that woman's sexual hold on man which, as Kochkaryov sees it, he suffers under, is a 'devilish' aspect of their nature:

> As though they only had nice little hands! They've got. . . . Well, what's the use of talking – the devil

alone knows what they haven't got.

And there are always the children . . . Kochkaryov adds a further bait to the marriage trap with the tempting prospect of a whole array of little despatch clerks, just like Podkolyosin, and the spitting image of their procreator. Even the production of children has become an aspect of sameness, just as the litany of the names of the Charity Commissioner's children in *The Government Inspector* culminates in 'Perepetuya'. The images of children are contained in the splintered reflections of Podkolyosin, in the smashed mirror on the floor, just like the smashed glass in *Gamblers*. The production of identical, and destroyed, images of self has become the substitute for the realization of the full multiplicity of the potential of self in life. At the same time, retaining a hold on one's singleness is an aspect of security. This is as true for Agafya as it is for Podkolyosin. As she approaches marriage, she begins to imagine whole hosts of Podkolyosins appearing before her eyes. She tries to grab them and put them in her reticule but the essential Podkolyosin keeps escaping. To marry, on these terms, is to risk being put in the bag. Podkolyosin resists by jumping out of the window.

There is an emphasis on fear. When the first suitor, Yaichnitsa, arrives, the women peer through the keyhole. Their vision reveals a giant before whom they flee in terror. When Agafya, apparently under the spell of Kochkaryov, refuses Yaichnitsa, the latter advances on her threateningly like an ogre. She screams and flees, as does her aunt. They behave as if they have momentarily seen past the civil servant to another level of reality – to the image in the distorting mirror. Gogol provides us with a clue. Just as Podkolyosin is, ironically, a professional 'expeditor' (someone who expedites, that is, a despatch clerk), so Yaichnitsa is called an 'executor' (someone who 'executes', that is, carries out executive tasks). During the course of re-writing the play Gogol changed Yaichnitsa's patronymic from 'Petrovich' to 'Pavlich'. In ordinary conversation the latter sounds like *palach*, which is the Russian for 'executioner', and should be emphasized as such in production. We then recognize the degrees of violence below the surface of the drama and not just in the images of consumption. Yaichnitsa is like an ogre who is going to devour Agafya. Onuchkin describes his own father as having been a 'monster' and, in strangely masochistic fashion, wishes he had been whipped more as a child. The aunt describes Agafya's father as having had 'hands as big as buckets' and says that Agafya's mother would have lived longer if she had not been beaten so often. In an argument about whether a nobleman has more power than a merchant, Fyokla declares that a nobleman can cut off a merchant's head; to which the aunt counters, comically: 'But then the merchant can complain to the police.' The outer world is full of terrors, both physical and mental. It is little surprise that people prefer to stay at home or seek what they see as the safe refuge of marriage. But, no matter where you hide or retreat to, the ultimate realities will seek you out despite all your efforts and assert themselves in distorted and grotesque form.

There is someone in the play who claims to have encountered the outside world and to have weathered its storms – Zhevakin. He has recently returned from a trip around the world and makes his entrance – covered in cobwebs and dust. The road he has travelled along that morning is overgrown with grass. Nobody makes journeys any more. 'Oh, Auntie, it's "The Road" again', complains Agafya to her aunt as she tries to discover her destiny in the cards. How has the experience of travel affected

Zhevakin? The only change appears to be that the seams have gone on his jacket. He might just as well have stayed at home gathering dust in a cupboard, like the mummy in Strindberg's *The Ghost Sonata*. He has even, we learn, paid a visit to Gogol's beloved Italy, where he confuses Venice with Sicily and imagines everyone speaks French. Everything, in his description, loses meaning – language, nationhood, experience. People become reduced to gibbering apes, like the Russian and English sailors who are described as not needing language to communicate, as they can manage quite happily with signs and noises. Gogol's beloved ideal – the eternal feminine – is also trampled metaphorically underfoot in Zhevakin's description. The high becomes reduced to the low. The 'dark beauties' stand on a roof balcony (admittedly not very high up but at least he is forced to raise his eyes aloft) but the terms Zhevakin uses to describe the 'rosebud' are nauseating, and the roofs turn out to be flat anyway, 'as flat as this floor' as Zhevakin says. The word for floor and the word for sex *(pol)* are the same. This so-called 'farce' asks despairing questions about the nature of reality, about identity, about language. What are people? Are they nothing? Are they the language they speak? Are they animals? Do their names mean anything? Are they no more than the bits of paper which Agafya cuts up and shuffles in a bag to make one whole person? This seems to be her ideal. Her dream amounts to a puppet-like, identikit version of her perfect man where the nose is taken from x, the hair from y and the feet from z. Put them together and you arrive at . . . what? In the deepest recesses of his consciousness, Podkolyosin tries to escape narrow and partial definitions and attempts to reach out to wider meanings and significances. But beyond the boundary of marriage lies the uncharted territory of tempest and madness, as well as ideal love and ideal beauty. To attain this other world is, literally, a leap in the dark and is best made, as Podkolyosin recognizes, with a hat on, although that will afford little protection 'out there'.

However, the possibility of the existence of human spirit *is* there and the metaphor of flight serves to characterize it. But all these birds lack tail feathers, are 'plucked', or are so 'weighed down' that they are unable to take flight. The leap through the window is the nearest anyone gets to it. All aspiration ends with marriage – for property, for sex, for social advancement. This is the level of the striving and the extent of the perception. It is derisory, but this is not all there is, Gogol seems to be saying. It is merely a diminished version of the real possibilities, just as marriage, true marriage, is the final unity of all diversity, the introduction of harmony into a world whose reality resides at any point between two diametrically opposite poles. The dialectic of oppositions needs to be recognised and a unity striven for, towards the higher end of these polarities. Marriage is, indeed, everything. But here, it is nothing.

There is also another way of reconciling opposites. There is a conversation, worthy of Ionesco, between Agafya and Podkolyosin in which they are getting to know each other. In the middle of a hiatus in the conversational flow, something escapes from Podkolyosin like an emanation from his subconscious and its significance escapes both of them. Apropos of nothing in particular he says:

How bold the Russian people are.

Even the resourceful Agafya is thrown by this apparent *non sequitur*. He has to explain himself:

Gogol's Plays 1832-1842

Workers. Standing right at the very top . . . I was walking past a house and a plasterer was plastering (*shchekaturschik shtukaturit*), not afraid of anything . . .

This may be a definition of limited consciousness but, in this world, it is also a considerable achievement. No fear of heights; no problems of identify; a modest unity of opposites brought about in the act of work itself and at a point higher than the floor from which Podkolyosin leaps. But, perhaps, Gogol might say, we all, finally, live where Agafya and everyone else appears to live, *na Peskom* (on sand) and *v pereulke* (in a narrow alley).

Among the many interesting Soviet productions of the play, the most notorious was that staged by the so-called Factory Of The Eccentric Actor (FEKS) on 25 September 1922, directed by the young iconoclasts Grigori Kozintsev and Leonid Trauberg. The production was conceived very much in the spirit of the Russian Futurist movement and orientated towards what was described as the 'Americannization' of culture, combining the rhythms of the jazz and machine age with the dynamic of early cinema. The FEKS poster, advertizing the production, read:

AMERIKA VORWÄRTS! AMERICA FORWARD! AMERIQUE EN AVANT!

IN THE PRODUCTION – OPERETTA, MELODRAMA, FARCE, FILM, CIRCUS, VARIETY, GUIGNOL, CHARLIE CHAPLIN AND THE LOVELY BETTY

DEMONSTRATION OF THE THEORY OF RELATIVITY OF PROFESSOR EINSTEIN

ELECTRIFICATION OF N. V. GOGOL ???

AFTER THE PRODUCTION A DISPUTE. . . .

Nikolai Gogol and Ivan Turgenev

The avant-garde, experimentalist approach was very much in tune with the spirit of post-revolutionary Russia following the Civil War and was influenced by, as well as competing with, the excitingly experimental work in a similar vein conducted by Sergei Eisenstein at the Proletkult Theatre, and Meyerhold at his State Theatre Workshop. In fact, the production of *Marriage* was given at the Proletkult Theatre, in Moscow, where audiences had already seen Eisenstein's version of Jack London's *The Mexican* and would shortly see his montage, modernist version of Ostrovski's *Enough Stupidity In Every Wise Man*.

The whole production consisted of a series of stunts, utilizing the means of circus, music-hall, acrobatics, and gymnastics, interspersed with jazz, marches, factory sirens and film sequences. Just as Meyerhold had introduced a clown, Lazarenko, into his 1921 revival of *Mystery-Bouffe*, so Kozintsev and Trauberg introduced the two popular circus performers Serge and Taurek into their production of *Marriage*. Now and again, a few isolated lines from the original play came through, but without any logical connection between them. As a first attempt at 'contemporization' of the classics, the production was a protest against the conservatism and academicism of the senior theatres and, as such, proved very influential in spawning a host of, often inferior, imitations. According to Serge, who took part in the performance:

> They brought chamber pots on the stage. They electrified Gogol by putting a plug and electric wire into his posterior. They played every possible rough trick on him and generally abused him.[11]

Yet another notorious production of *Marriage* was given on 29 January 1924, at the Moscow Art Theatre Third

Gogol's Plays 1832-1842

Studio, directed by the young Yuri Zavadski. The play's epigraph – 'An absolutely incredible incident in two acts' – was adopted as the keynote to a fantastic, unreal and mystical interpretation of the play, metamorphosed by the director into a nightmare. The stage was populated by terrifying mystical-caricatural figures. The servant, Stepan, and Kochkaryov were played in a manner suggestive of wild animals and were accompanied throughout by two mysterious *doppelgänger*. The production was described as having a strong expressionist element. The actors gesticulated, at times, like marionettes and, at others, employed whispers instead of ordinary speech. Everything was slowed down, lines were long-drawn-out, and exaggerated pauses were introduced. Symbolic music by N. I. Sizov accompanied the action and accentuated its mood. S. P. Isakov supplied expressionistic decor, which was carried over into the costuming. Lighting effects caused the setting to seem to dematerialize before the eyes of the audience.[12] The production was, generally speaking, negatively reviewed and was even described as 'class-alien bourgeois mysticism'.[13] But, in many respects, Zavadski would appear to have sensed certain truths about the play which tend to be ignored.

Both these productions may be said to have owed something to the pioneering spirit of the Gaideburov Travelling Popular Theatre before the revolution. In the summer of 1916, the Gaideburov troupe staged *Marriage*, in a production by A. A. Bryantsev. It was dedicated to the memory of A. E. Martynov, who acted in the play's first production, and was conceived in the manner of the then popular and influential Symbolist school. Podkolyosin was interpreted as a positive figure seen against a background of typically Gogolian *poshlost*.[14] Gaideburov, who acted Podkolyosin, played him as a Russian Hamlet, noting that this comparison had been made by Apollon Grigoryev in 1859. Podkolyosin's sufferings were moved to the centre of the production and were seen to stand for the sufferings of the Russian intelligentsia, lost in contradictions, and revealed in 'impressionistic psychological' form.[15]

The play has constantly been revived in the Soviet Union and a recent production of note has been that of the Malaya Bronnaya Theatre, in Moscow, directed by Anatoli Efros, and seen at the Edinburgh Festival in 1978. In placing the problem of women and the myth of marriage at the centre of the production (in the shape of Agafya Tikhonovna) Efros caused Gogol's play to lose:

. . . its purely burlesque aspect . . . acquiring a seriousness (without earnestness) and an impact (without overstatement) for which the term 'tragi-comedy' is most suitable.[16]

5
'The Government Inspector'

In a letter to Pushkin dated 7 October 1835, Gogol begged him to supply an anecdote which he could use for the plot of a five-act comedy he was 'trembling' to write, and which would be funnier than the devil itself. The plot is well-known. The mayor and officials of an out-of-the-way provincial town receive warning by letter of the imminent arrival of a government inspector from the capital who is travelling incognito. An impoverished clerk from St Petersburg, who is holed up at the local inn unable to pay his bills because he has lost his money at cards, is mistaken for the government inspector and treats the respect he is accorded as long-overdue recognition of his worth. Within twenty-four hours he realises this is a case of mistaken identity but not before he gets drunk at a reception and indulges in a ludicrous feat of boasting, accepts bribes from the local town officials and flirts with the mayor's wife and daughter, even concluding an engagement with the latter. He decides to beat a hasty retreat and, immediately following his departure, a letter he has written to a friend in St Petersburg is unsealed by the postmaster, exposing the clerk for the person he is and also exposing the self-deception of the townspeople. In this final moment of revelation, when scapegoats are being sought, the arrival of the real government inspector is announced.

Signs of vaudeville are evident in the early versions of *The Government Inspector* (*Revizor*) where Khlestakov (*khlestat'* = to whip, with a secondary meaning of 'to tell lies' or 'talk nonsense'), is called Skakunov (*skatat'* = to caper or to gallop). In the second version his name was changed to Perepelkin (*perepel* = a quail; *perepelenat'* = to change a nappy). Gogol also used word games very much in the manner of vaudeville. He has Khlestakov explain the term 'comedy' to Marya Antonovna by saying that 'comedy . . . is exactly the same as artillery', for no better reason than that they both end in 'y'. The under-officer's widow ends her complaint about having been whipped by the mayor with an offer to show her behind with the incriminating marks on it to the 'high dignitary'. Many of these cruder elements were progressively eliminated, including a reference to Pushkin's creativity depending on his intake of rum. Jokes about Bobchinski's red nose also disappeared, as did references to the mayor's fat one.

There were surprisingly few problems with censorship. The play was written very rapidly and was first submitted to the censor on 27 February 1836. The first performance was two months later, on 19 April. An interesting point is that, even after the publication of the 'canonical' text of the play, which was considerably different from the 1836 version, the 'correct' version was not permitted performance until the 1870s. In 1836, Oldekop, the censor, merely required that references to the mayor's culpability be toned down, and that there be no references to the church

'The Government Inspector'

or the Order of St Vladimir. Mistaking the sergeant's wife for an officer's wife, the censor also requested that she be removed, although the reference to her having been whipped was, for some reason, retained.

The first reading of the play took place at the house of the poet, V. A. Zhukovski, in the presence of Pushkin, another poet Prince Vyazemski, and Count Velgorski. Gogol's reading was received with delight. As Vyazemski wrote to a friend:

> He reads masterfully and provokes wave upon wave of laughter. I am not sure the play will not lose something in performance, for few actors will be able to play it as he reads it.[1]

Turgenev's account of the famous occasion in 1851 when Gogol read the play for the benefit of the Moscow actors, captures some of this quality:

> . . . he wanted to show the actor who played Khlestakov how one had to perform that really difficult scene. [The lying scene in Act 3.] In Gogol's interpretation it seemed natural and truthful to me. Khlestakov is carried away by the strangeness of his position, by his surroundings and by his own frivolous nimble-mindedness; he knows that he is telling lies and --- believes his own lies: it is a sort of ecstasy, a sort of inspiration, a story-teller's enthusiasm --- it is not an ordinary sort of lie, not an ordinary sort of bragging. He was himself "carried away". . . . That was the impression produced by Khlestakov's monologue as read by Gogol.[2]

In 1836, Gogol had also read the play to the cast at the

Alexandrinski Theatre. With the exception of Sosnitski, who acted the mayor, the actors were not impressed. Gogol attended rehearsals with the director, Khrapovitski, but the actors ignored his suggestions and adopted the well-worn conventions of vaudeville. The audience at the first night were bewildered. They had come expecting a farce and that was certainly reflected in most of the acting, but the play itself was so life-like and Sosnitski's interpretation of the mayor so realistic that they were disturbed. Reaction varied from act to act. The conclusion was greeted with virtually unanimous indignation. Gogol left the theatre and did not respond to the cries of 'Author!' from his friends in the audience. Critical reaction among the conservatives was hostile. The play was considered an insult and a travesty although the Tsar, it was claimed, had been heard to say that he had enjoyed it. Gogol was described as 'an enemy of Russia' and it was even proposed that he be sent in shackles to Siberia. Prince Vyazemski wrote:

> The comedy was acknowledged by many people as a liberal manifesto.... a political bombshell flung at society under the guise of a comedy.[3]

One Prince Tsitsiyanov hurriedly wrote a riposte in the shape of a play called *The Real Government Inspector*, published in July 1836, in which it transpired that the real government inspector had been in town all along, keeping an eye on things. At the end, he punished the officials, sent Khlestakov into the army and married the mayor's daughter. An unsuccessful attempt was made to stage the play on the same bill as Gogol's as an afterpiece.

Nobody understood Gogol or his intentions, neither friends nor enemies. He wrote mournfully to his friend

'The Government Inspector'

Shchepkin:

> Now I see what it means to be a comedy writer . . . I am appalled by the obtuse irritability which pervades all classes of our society . . . To call a crook a crook is to undermine the foundations of our State.[4]

Everybody was against him, he said, the police, the merchants, the literary people. Yet, despite the cry that he held nothing sacred, everybody was flocking to the theatre and it was impossible to get tickets for the fourth performance. Gogol recognized that, without the Tsar's intercession (he had apparently approved the play for performance in the first instance), it would undoubtedly have been banned.

The central critical divisions arose over the question of whether the play was a 'satire' (the reactionary view) or a 'gentle comedy' (the view of the play's supporters). The critic O. Senkovski felt that, instead of producing a comedy of morals, Gogol had written an anecdotal work in which all the characters were either swindlers or fools and that there was a total absence of honest people when, in reality, people are a mixture of the bad and the good. His advice to Gogol consisted of a number of revisions, the most significant of which was to have him extend Khlestakov's stay in town, meet a noblewoman and flirt with her and thus encourage the jealousy of the mayor's daughter. Their amusing rivalry would then constitute an aspect of genuine comedy which the play at present lacked.

N. Polevoy described it as a straightforward farce without any development, plot or purpose. He derided those critics who saw anything significant in the play in the form of artistic merit or of valid social criticism; it was simply full of monstrous grotesques, both absurd and funny, reminiscent of a Russian folk tale. This kind of criticism was countered by P. Vyazemski, who distinguished between farce and comedy, finding very little that was farcical in the play, except for the collapsing door at the inn. Gogol, he declared, had established a new genre which was neither low farce nor high comedy in the manner of Molière. Defending certain improbabilities and inconsistencies in the plotting, Vyazemski stressed that what was involved was not literal truth but psychological truth and that, in the latter sense, the crucial factor was that characters' reactions were determined by the dominance of an all-embracing sense of fear. This was precisely Belinski's view, for whom Khlestakov was 'the phantom shadow of the mayor's guilty conscience'. In fact, Belinski considered the play a model creation of a genre, taking his example from the Platonic dialogues where Socrates points to the inner connections between tragedy and comedy.[5]

V. Androsov, writing in the *Moscow Observer* in 1836, stoutly defended the play. There was nothing special in exciting laughter for its own sake, the critic said, but when the arousal of laughter had a specific polemical purpose and directed attention to social abuses, then it had beneficial effects. Nobody wanted to attack authority or righteousness as such, but if those principles were simply masks for wrong-doing, that merely served to undermine respect for order. In laughing at the judge or the mayor one was not laughing at Authority or Justice but at their perversions. In *The Government Inspector*, he felt, it was wrong to look for the kind of external truth which it is accustomed to demand from comedies. In this play, there was the inner truth of the Idea and this had the effect of

'The Government Inspector'

placing the comedy high among the small number of truly original dramatic compositions.[6]

Gogol had more to say about this play than almost anything else he wrote. The aesthetic ideas propounded in *Conversation After The Play* seem to be close to those of Androsov. The latter contrasts the 'bitterness of satire' with the 'merriment of comedy', and suggests that the conflict between the two can be resolved as a move is made from external truth towards the internal truth of ideas. In Gogol's remarks in his *Advance Notice To Actors* on how the play should be acted, there is a sense that he shares, with Belinski, a feeling for the unity of comedy and tragedy as well as a belief that true comedy arises from the seriousness with which the characters play their parts. Again, like Belinski, he emphasizes the importance of the motivating force of fear as psychological justification for the verisimilitude of the events, and also as motivating force for the characters. It is also, as he points out, the power of a general fear which has the effect of converting Khlestakov into a comic character. He answers critics of the final scene by stressing its seriousness. The position of many of the characters has become 'almost tragic'.[7]

Some of these aspects had been present in Shchepkin's interpretation of the mayor at the first Moscow performance of the play, in May 1836, with D. T. Lenski as Khlestakov. During the scene at the inn, quaking with fear, Shchepkin uttered the lines about his wife and children with tears in his voice, an expression of woe on his face and a trembling lip. A swindler was endowed with pathos in a moment. His performance was one of undaunted energy, creating the impression of someone at constant odds with his enemies. At the end, the feeling was that he had been deceived but not beaten, like someone fanatical and maniacal fighting phantoms of the imagination.[8]

Where *Gamblers* and *Marriage* appear marked in most treatments of Gogol's work by a dearth of critical attention, *The Government Inspector*, by contrast, has exacted its full measure. There exists a wealth of material in both Russian and English devoted to this outstanding comedy. Following the important groundwork laid by Belinski, Chernyshevski and others, Gogol criticism did not become an 'industry' until about fifty years after his death when one line of critical approach, which might be called the 'quasi mystical', was established by Dmitri Merezhkovski. Merezhkovski's 1906 article *Gogol And The Devil*, whilst not itself advancing a particularly 'mystical' interpretation of *The Government Inspector*, may be said to have provided a platform for more 'formalist' conceptions of the play (for example, Nabokov's chapter 'The Government Spectre' in his *Nikolai Gogol*) in which the play's symbolic form and content are seen to far outreach any relevance the play might have to the social world in which it was produced. In actual fact what Merezhkovski has to say tends more towards emphasizing the play's realism. The fog which Zemlyanika refers to in Act 5 and which seems to envelop the play and cloud the characters' judgement (like an emanation of evil, in some criticisms), Merezhkovski relates directly to St Petersburg '. . . that most ghostly, foggy, fantastic of all cities. . . .'[9] The devil turns out to be the incarnation of ordinariness, who 'goes around in an ordinary tail-coat'. The evil in the play consists of banality, in the absence of anything tragic, in the smallest rather than in the greatest things. Khlestakov is an incarnation of these qualities, as light and insubstantial as a feather which accounts for his 'phantasmagorical' aspect.

'The Government Inspector'

In a letter to S. T. Aksakov, in 1844, Gogol described this kind of 'devil':

> He's like a minor civil servant who turns up in some town ostensibly to conduct an investigation. He'll throw dust in everyone's eyes, give everyone a dressing-down, and start shouting his head off. All you have to do is tremble a bit and draw back, and he'll pluck up his courage. But the moment you make a move toward him, he'll tuck his tail between his legs. We're the ones who make a giant out of him; actually, he is the Devil knows what.[10]

Khlestakov's quality is precisely a lack of definition, inconclusiveness, but at the same time he is an emanation of what might be called the 'consciousness of the race'. In other times, in other eras, people of heroic stature were 'made' by the people as projections of a collectivity. In modern times, out of their fear and mean-spiritedness, they can only produce a petty-devil. Khlestakov is a *minor* poet, a *minor* aspirant, which the scale of his flights of fancy, as well as his eventual flight in the troika, serve to demonstrate. The ceiling of his aspiration and the reach of his imaginative heights are low. In this context, his recitation of a Lomonosov poem about human fate is a form of sacrilege; his naming of Pushkin, *The Marriage of Figaro* and *Yuri Miloslavski*, (an inferior work by Zagoskin) in the same breath, is part of the universal level of banality and sameness. Nothing can be qualitatively distinguished in a world which has become devoid of value; in its place has been substituted a vulgar epicureanism, whose highest aspiration is, in Khlestakov's words, 'to pluck the blooms of pleasure'.

The Symbolist, Vyacheslav Ivanov, stressed the social function of the comedy, even going so far as to compare

Gogol with Aristophanes.[11] He also points to a didactic element in the play's 'mediaeval' traits, which make of it 'an edifying parable in didactic form', creating an echo of Gogol's notion of the theatre as a pulpit. V. Gippius, one of the outstanding Soviet commentators on Gogol's drama, states that the play is about official abuses and the concept of true service to the state, but insists that there is no didactic purpose behind Gogol's choice of specific social and professional roles for the characters.[12]

Opposed to the whole thrust of criticism mentioned above is that of Nabokov, who sees the play as a gigantic linguistic conjuring trick which 'begins with a blinding flash of lightning and ends in a thunderclap'.[13] For A. de Jonge, the character of Khlestakov 'has sinister not to say diabolic connotations'. This does not seem to be in Merezhkovski's sense of the diabolic but rather possessing something malignantly mysterious. Zemlyanika's remark to the effect that: 'It's as if some kind of fog confused us, it was the devil's doing', is equated with Osip's 'more sinister, if less obvious' remark in answer to Khlestakov's query as to why he is not being treated like other travellers at the inn: 'But of course they are not like you'. De Jonge also makes some interesting observations about the 'mediaeval' elements in the play which relate to allegory and parable and supply it with its sense of good and evil.[14]

Gogol expressed his own idea of what he was trying to do in *The Government Inspector* when writing *An Author's Confession* in 1847:

> I decided to gather in one pile all the bad in Russia of which I was then aware, all the injustices which are committed in those places, and on those occasions where justice above all is demanded of man, and at the same time, to laugh at everything.[15]

'The Government Inspector'

A further statement of Gogol's intention was also made, in retrospect, in his short didactic conversation piece *The Dénouement of the Government Inspector*, where the town is described as symbolizing man's soul, the corrupt officials his base passions, and the figure of the *Revizor* man's awakening conscience. We would do well not to minimize the importance of this statement even if we do not take it too literally.

Gogol's reputation as a world dramatist rests almost entirely on *The Government Inspector*, a play which, it is generally acknowledged, is very difficult to translate adequately and is, therefore, only known in, at best, unsatisfactory translations. It is, therefore, worth noting the variations in the kinds of language which the characters are given in the original – for example, the limited cunning and portentousness of the mayor's speech combined with a terrific command of expletive; the postmaster's naïveté and slow-wittedness which are part of his phraseology; Anna Andreyevna's mannered preciosity mixed with vulgar colloquialism. None before Gogol, and few since, have managed to weld colloquial Russian into such a uniquely expressive and essentially dramatic medium, possessing the power and resourcefulness of verse.

The beginnings of Gogol's plays are always significant. This comedy begins with a figure of Authority surrounded by its satellite representatives of Enlightenment, Health, Justice and Charity. The play also begins with a characteristic set of repetitions. The word *revizor* is repeated four times in the first four lines and the word is associated with something unknown, 'incognito', and secret. The mayor then goes on to talk about a dream. The world of dream is especially significant for Gogol as it stands opposed to the surface world of calculation, time, money, cause and effect. Even someone like the mayor still possesses the power to dream and, through it, to penetrate to another kind of reality even though, in doing so, that reality begins to take on overtones of the comic grotesque. Nevertheless, the dream stands for something significant. The key terms of the account of the dream are 'intuition', 'night', 'blackness' and 'rats'. Superficially comic, it alerts our attention to a deeper level of nightmare with connotations of finality, corpses, nothingness. Then follows an interesting stage direction as the mayor 'mutters in a low voice as he runs through the letter'. Much depends on the way this is treated in performance but there is a strong suggestion that Gogol intends it to sound like a reading from a holy text, muttered in church, with the significant sections emphasized: 'to inform you' (repeated) 'the whole province . . . especially our district'. Another interesting stage direction follows: 'He raises his finger aloft significantly.' Again, depending on performance, there is a clear indication that this is both a naturalistic gesture and, in another key, is also the finger of judgement raised slowly over the heads of those present which can descend 'Shast!', just like that, as he says later when the doors burst open to admit Bobchinski and Dobchinski, but also, through them, the spectre of Judgement. The key words and phrases which follow seem clearly related to final judgement and death. The talk is of 'sins'. He can 'arrive at any time' – 'incognito'. These, it would seem, are the parameters of the play – this life seen in relation to the absolute fact of death and judgement. If this is the case, then the pattern of the play is perfectly formed. It begins with the finger raised and ends with the finger brought down, crushingly, on the quick and the dead.

Another part of the pattern is also present in this opening. The 'truth' is received in the form of the written word and is accepted as 'biblical' truth (Chmykhov's letter). It is also dissolved through the written word (Khlestakov's letter). The play is testament to the extraordinary power which the written word possesses. It travels to the ends of the earth (by post). Words, when written down, have almost magical powers: 'Ah well, if you've got a letter – there won't be war with the Turks'. Therefore, the *quality* of the written word is important. Chmykhov in his letter, the correspondents whose secrets the postmaster shares, Tryapichkin, even Khlestakov, partake of its power and its magic but only succeed in distorting and perverting its essence. The Bible is the word incarnate, the intermediary between this world and the next, with the priest a kind of spiritual postmaster. But instead of a 'visionary' we have a 'spier' in the figure of Ivan Kuzmich Shpyokin.

Gogol presents us with yet another version of the division of labour. Health is the province of Gibner (*gibnut'* = to perish). Education is the province of Khlopov (*khlopat'* = to slam or slap). 'Caritas' is the province of Zemlyanika. Justice is the province of Lyapkin- Tyapkin. 'Language' also seems to be the province of Gibner, as the mayor suggests when he asks that a sign be placed above each patient's bed on which something should be written in Latin, or some such language: 'That's your department', he says, addressing the doctor. It is interesting that, in the early versions of the play, Gibner could at least speak. Here he, the linguist, can only utter inarticulate sounds. It is not just a joke at the expense of Germans who cannot speak Russian. The Healer is called Christian, but his patients are dying in droves. (They 'get well like flies'.) It is the doctor who should be in charge of what the mayor describes as 'internal arrangements' – that area which, in the letter from Chmykhov, is said to contain the 'little sins'. The words which Gogol carefully chooses establish a spiritual dimension to the world which is unfolding and also point to the significance of the doctor, whose virtual nonexistence becomes a spiritual vacuum at the centre of the play. They also point to a total lack of a spiritual dimension within the inhabitants of the drama as a whole. There is not a man 'without sin', says the mayor and accuses the judge of never going to church, whereas he, the mayor, is 'firm in my faith'; this invokes a typically Gogolian irony of 'going to church every Sunday' – an act of meaningless ritual, habit and superstition.

Education – the world of the great teachers, which includes Christ, as well as Plato and Socrates – has evolved (seemingly via the judge's explanation of the Creation) to produce a group of grotesques who are only capable of pulling faces. The mayor's description of their activities suggests that the words they use have become a dead letter, meaningless. They mug, grimace, smooth their beards from under their cravats and, in a marvellous parody of bygone heroism, imitate the actions of Alexander the Great by smashing school furniture. As the mayor remarks prophetically, 'the devil knows what will become of it'.

His warning about what might flow from that 'damned incognito' sounds like a roll-call at the Last Judgement as each is called before some higher authority before being consigned to the flames: 'And who is the judge? – Lyapkin-Tyapkin – Bring forth Lyapkin-Tyapkin! . . .' and so on. The devil is already potentially present, unnoticed, amidst the general disorder in the judicial offices, or in the squalor of the Charitable Institution, in the ignorance and disarray of the classroom. He has entered the Postal Department through the half-opened flap of a letter. He may be a petty devil, but the evils

'The Government Inspector'

which flow from his admission grow to mammoth proportions. The implication is that the smaller involves the greater, not only in the abstract terms of good and evil, but also in the social pattern in which this town is connected to the larger unit of St Petersburg. It is the evil which emanates from 'the internal condition', social and personal, which knows no boundaries.

Gogol appears to imply that the admission of evil carries retribution with it. Once the hunting whip has been allowed into the office to a place on top of the cupboard of official papers, this cannot just be tidied away temporarily and then put back again once there has been an inspection. The whip carries retribution with it. Gogol describes it as an *okhotny arapnik*, literally 'a hunting whip', but he means it to stand for Khlestakov (the whipper). He is the retributive hunting *arapnik*, already peeping out of the files and half-opened letters ready to give the perpetrators of folly a sound swingeing which cannot be forgotten as soon as he leaves.

The arrival of Bobchinski and Dobchinski introduces another theme in the play, one which connects internal and external worlds and which relates to the health of the individual and the health of society – that of food. The world of *The Government Inspector* consists of the grossly over-fed and the starving. Gogol refers in his character delineations at the beginning of the play to the 'potbellies' of Bobchinski and Dobchinski. The latter has a delicate stomach and needs to eat salmon. All the town officials are well-fed and the mayor's dream of St Petersburg embroiders a fantasy of even rarer delicacies. Khlestakov is starving and indulges in the fantasies of the hungry – soup from Paris and a 700-rouble melon. Osip is also starving and, as is clear, usually has to make do with his master's leavings. His fantasy of St Petersburg life also includes food. The play is full of references to food and drink and over-indulgence, so that virtually all the town officials become figures in a mediaeval panorama depicting gluttony. The one exception is Luka Lukich, whose nerves have caused him to waste away. The stomach, *zheludka*, becomes a centre of well-being. Dobchinski's 'disorder' is seen to derive from over-eating. This is paralleled by a form of mental disorder in Bobchinski, derived from an overactive, because starved, imagination which mistakes impoverished clerks for dignitaries and which hungers for the imaginative food of other worlds, but can only peer through cracks in doors (as in the scene at the inn) a metaphorical equivalent of peeking under letter flaps. In his wish that Khlestakov remind the Tsar of his existence, Bobchinski connects us with the themes of hunger and, especially, neglect. In an Act 4 stage direction added by Gogol to the final version of the play, the hands of petitioners wielding their paper complaints and seeking redress of grievances, are seen through a window. This is then succeeded by a vision of universal poverty, violence, starvation and neglect as the rear doors open to reveal a figure 'in a frieze greatcoat with an unshaved chin, a swollen lip and a bandaged cheek'. To which Gogol added: 'Behind him is seen a vista of others'.

Khlestakov connects the internal and external worlds in arriving from outside. He is, so to speak, consumed by the town and gives rise to internal disorder. Fear begins to take over from the moment Bobchinski and Dobchinski have told of their encounter at the inn in Act 1. The mayor begins to echo Bobchinski's mistake of taking one thing for another. First of all he instructs the orderly to tell everyone to 'grab a street', when he means 'a broom'. The judge has already said that the chaos in the judicial department is such that truth cannot be distinguished from

1. Marya Savina as Marya Antonovna in Gogol's *The Government Inspector*, Aleksandrinski Theatre, St Petersburg, 1881

2. A scene from Act 5 of *The Government Inspector*, Moscow Art Theatre, 1908

3. Michael Chekhov as Khlestakov in *The Government Inspector*, Moscow Art Theatre, 1921

4. Erast Garin as Khlestakov in *The Government Inspector*, Meyerhold Theatre, Moscow, 1926

5. Alec Guinness as Khlestakov in *The Government Inspector*, New Theatre, London, 1948. Photograph: John Vickers

6. *L to R:* Olga Yakovleva as Agafya, Mikhail Kozakov as Kochkaryov and Nikolai Volkov as Podkolyosin in Gogol's *Marriage*, Malaya Dronnaya Theatre, Moscow, 1975

7. *L:* K. Stanislavski *and R:* V. Kachalov as Rakitin in the 1909 Moscow Art Theatre production of Turgenev's *A Month In The Country*

8. Design by M. V. Dobuzhinski for Act 1 of *A Month In The Country*, Moscow Art Theatre, 1909

9. *L to R:* Valerie Taylor as Natalya Petrovna and Isolde Denham as Vera in *A Month In The Country*, St James's Theatre, London, 1943

10. Angela Baddeley as Natalya Petrovna and Michael Redgrave as Rakitin in *A Month In The Country*, Old Vic Theatre, London, 1950

11. K. Stanislavski and his wife, M. Lilina, as Count Lyubin and Darya Ivanovna in Turgenev's *A Provincial Lady*, Moscow Art Theatre, 1912

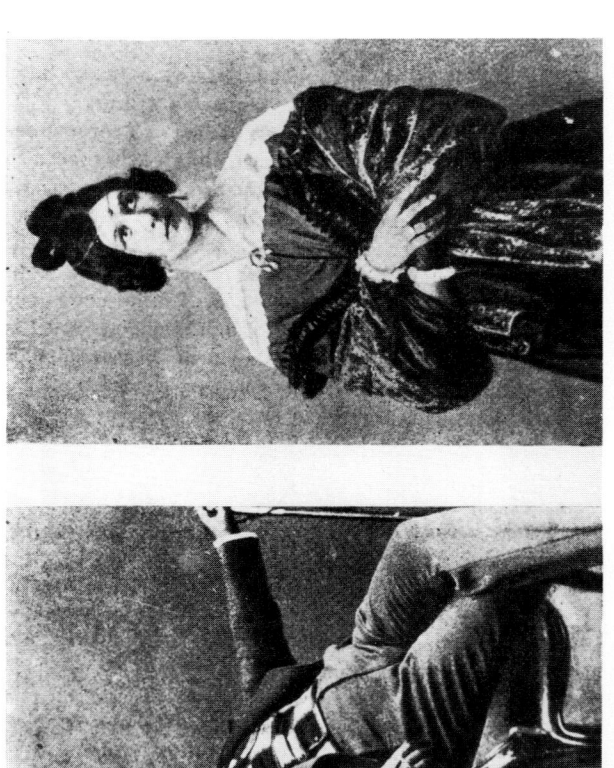

12. L. M. Leonidov as Tropachov and L. M. Koreneva as Olga Petrovna in Turgenev's *The Parasite*, Moscow Art Theatre, 1912

falsehood. This symptomatic casualness is shown to have wider and far-reaching consequences, once again of a retributive nature. The mayor's *lapsus linguae* is followed by the famous moment of the hatbox, donned in mistake for a hat, which was retained from the first version of the play and which most commentators describe as part of a tendency on Gogol's part to rely for comic effect on elements of vaudeville. The same is said of the collapsing door at the inn. Nothing could be further from the truth. The mayor's mistaking the hatbox for the hat is a metaphorical demonstration of his tendency, under the influence of fear, to be unable to distinguish with his customary certainty between what is true and what is false. The 'vaudeville' stunt anticipates the confrontation with Khlestakov and justifies, psychologically, his acceptance of this 'hatbox' of a clerk for the 'hat' of a government inspector, despite all appearances to the contrary. 'The box is a box. The devil take it', says the mayor, when we have just seen him take it for something else.

'Go and look through a crack and find out everything', shrieks Anna Andreyevna to the serving girl, Avdotya. 'In two hours' time we shall know everything', says her daughter. This is an extraordinary world in which the secret of the universe seems available to those who diligently peer under letter flaps, through a crack in the door, or through the keyhole, or for whom minutes and hours are ample time for ultimate revelation. Bobchinski peers round a door at the inn and glimpses a meeting between two 'christian mortals', in the mayor's words. What is Khlestakov frightened of at first? It is the turning of the door-handle, indicated in a stage direction. He is terrified of the door which opens into himself, into his own emptiness. 'I'm a . . . I'm . . . I'm . . .' he stutters inarticulately as he searches for self-definition The mayor is more confident of his own inner identity, which he controls by being two people at once. He believes he can shuttle between the two versions of himself, the inner private person and the outer public person, and still retain control of truth and illusion. Instead, the opposite happens. Appearance and reality grow further and further apart, as do the two sides of his nature.

At the end of the scene between Khlestakov and the mayor, there is another of those strange moments in this extraordinary play when, as Dobchinski goes to open the door:

> . . . it tears itself off its hinges and Bobchinski, who has been listening from the other side, flies on to the stage together with it ['her' in Russian, that is, the door]. Everyone lets out a shout.

It is very like the final dumb scene, which is prefaced by a simultaneous exhalation of breath from everyone on stage in response to the shock, but here the action continues. What *has* happened? This is no vaudeville stunt. While the door has fallen off its hinges because of Bobchinski's weight against it, at the same time some external force has entered the play. It is so powerful it resembles a gigantic blast which not only tears the door off its hinges but lifts Bobchinski up bodily and hurls him, and the door he has been making love to, physically on to the stage. The only sign that anything out of the ordinary has happened is a 'small bruise – just above the nose', and the conventional cure is one of Christian Ivanovich's plasters. But, just as if what has been admitted through the crack in the door has struck everyone a massive blow on the head, everything which follows takes place in a daze of confusion which the 'Healer' is powerless to minister to. The devil himself has

'*The Government Inspector*'

entered the play and blinded everyone. His mark is there, on the floor, 'spread out, like the devil knows what', as the mayor remarks to the contrite Bobchinski, indicating the place of his 'fall' and the seemingly indelible stain of its sprawled, and spreading, image. It is from this dark room, under the stairs, that the devil himself emerges like a shadow presence accompanying all the characters and, like a shadow, is gigantic in proportion to the conventional size of the human figures.

An hour has passed between Acts 1 and 3 but, during the scene at the inn, time has stopped and people are frozen in an eternal moment, which anticipates the final tableau. Anna Andreyevna and Marya Antonovna have remained, seemingly immobile, at the window through which we are treated to a vision glimpsed on two levels – of a deserted street and of a dead world: '. . . there's not a soul about; as if everyone's dead'. The only sign of life is Dobchinski. Or *is* it Dobchinski? It is also a little man in a frock coat, the shape of the contemporary devil – two things at the same time. 'Not very tall . . . in a frock coat . . . who is it?'

A note announces the 'government inspector's' arrival. It also pronounces judgement on the utter banality of a world where the mercy of God is conflated with pickled cucumbers and half a portion of caviare for 1 rouble 25 kopecks. Anna and Marya exit, and the sound of the rubbish they are talking wafts on from the wings. It is given physical embodiment in the rubbish which Misha sweeps on from off-stage, a manifestation of verbal trash in a world in which rubbish as a fact of existence, piled behind fences, overrunning the streets, begins to assume Beckettian proportions.

In his drunken speech, Khlestakov provides us with another vision of life – composed this time of an undifferentiated mass of insect-like creatures, buzzing and scratching, kept in thrall by a power which is itself experienced as a fact of nature, like the 'earthquake' produced by Khlestakov's presence among them. In their turn, the townspeople tremble before Khlestakov as before the might of nature itself. He, in his turn, is carried away on a self-abandoning tempest of rhetoric, striking fear and terror into the hearts of his auditors. It is both comic and terrifying. The devil has become, like Brecht's vision of an ambitious greengrocer in *Arturo Ui*, a little man with a moustache. 'It is terrifying, simply terrifying', says Artemi Filipovich, 'but I don't know why.' 'Oh, isn't he nice! What a dear little nose he's got. He's so sweet . . .' chorus Anna Andreyevna and Marya Antonovna. The significance of noses in Gogol's work does not need labouring.

The money in the judge's hand during the bribe scene is burning like fire. 'Oh God, I'm under the hand of judgement and the cart has come to take me away', he declares. People believe money can do anything. They can purchase their innocence, buy their exemption from judgement. Everything can become a transaction. One by one, the automatons, with their hands down the seams of their trousers in military fashion, file past and offer their financial sacrifice on the altar of officialdom to appease the Gods of Authority. Khlestakov can humiliate them, degrade them, insult them, flatter them – it makes no difference. Someone, like Artemi Filipovich, will seek the opportunity to turn the situation to his own advantage and betray his colleagues. He is the one with inheritors. 'What are your children called?' asks Khlestakov, and the vision of endless repetitions of little versions of Artemi Filipovich unfurls: 'Nikolai, Ivan, Elizaveta, Marya and Perepetuya' (and perpetua and perpetua and perpetua . . .). It is a vision of despair and Khlestakov finds it amusing – something for Tryapichkin to scribble about in the papers. And yet this is 'living', as Bobchinski wants the Tsar to note.

The attempted seduction of Marya Antonovna is in a different key. Something in her has not quite been destroyed. She feels insulted and humiliated and says so, if rather stupidly. The mother has long since crossed the divide between innocence and experience. What is a little potential incest with a son-in-law after all? As she declares, with devastating ambiguity when Khlestakov is on his knees before her: 'Get up, get up, the *pol* [floor/sex] here isn't clean'.

The 'phantasmagorical' figure of Khlestakov, like the personified image of deception, takes himself off in his troika, 'God knows whither'. This was how Gogol described him in the *Advance Notice To Actors*. This description has led to a tendency to see Khlestakov as something of a positive force, serving to reveal the town to itself, then taking off into the purer elements of air and space. Certainly he is going 'out there', but his armaments in his battle with the elements are money, sugar loaves, a silver tray and a bit of rope. His only protection is a cover and some straw as he submits to being packed into the troika like an egg in transit, fragile, and likely to be smashed by the first real bump. But he sits there, we imagine, like a dog in straw, or a pig in muck, as the coachman urges on his semi-ethereal steeds.

From one pig in muck Gogol turns to others, as the mayor and his wife contemplate wallowing in the swill of the Petersburg good life. The world is metamorphosing before our eyes into the one which the mayor subsequently sees, when enlightened, as composed of 'pigs' snouts'. The menagerie arrives to congratulate this forerunner of

Napolean Pig on his success. They give their blessing. At this juncture, with the departure of Khlestakov, the fog in which everyone has been groping is suddenly dispelled. It is signalled by the mayor's sneezing, twice. We are returned to the beginning of the play with the repetitions of *revizor*, prefixed, now by the negative *nye*, as the postmaster (prompted he suggests, by some 'devilish' power) leads us out of the maze through the reading of the unsealed letter.

The mayor, in a frenzy of passion, offers to do violence to his other self by threatening that self with his fist and grinding it under his heel. The process is cyclical and retributively self-destructive while embracing us all. 'What are you laughing at? You're laughing at yourselves.' The mayor makes the point that shadow and substance are inseperable. The final, alienated action is to look for scapegoats. These are physically objectified in the 'doubleness' of Dobchinski and Bobchinski, as the rest of the characters seek to avenge themselves on the false duality they have created and of which they are victims.

At this point, the emissary of Judgement appears and announces that the final reckoning, in the shape of the real government inspector, awaits them . . . at the very same inn which harboured Khlestakov! In this world there is judgement, of a sort, but no salvation. God, like the devil, is necessarily short in stature and dressed in a frock coat.

The twentieth century has seen some memorable productions of *The Government Inspector*, especially in Russia, none more so than that staged by Meyerhold at his theatre in Moscow, in 1926, which was probably more true to the spirit of Gogol's play than any production before or since.[16] Meyerhold's plans for staging the play had been formulated some twenty years previously when he first

'The Government Inspector'

read Merezhkovski's essay *Gogol and the Devil*. The production represented, in many respects, the apotheosis of all his experimental work in the theatre before and after the revolution, uniting elements of Commedia dell'Arte, symbolist and expressionist motifs, pantomime, harlequinade, techniques of oriental theatre, opera and ballet. It was staged with minute exactitude and ran almost throughout to musical accompaniment. The element of musicality underlay the choreography of the staging in a manner which harked back to Meyerhold's great production of Lermontov's *Masquerade* in 1917, in which the elaborate ball-scene had been stage-managed with the care of a ballet-master.

As self-styled 'author of the production', Meyerhold broke the five-act play down into fifteen scenes, each with its own title, wrote in lines and characters from Gogol's early drafts of the play and borrowed themes and characters from Gogol's other work. A particular, and notorious, instance was the role of a 'travelling companion' in the shape of an officer in uniform who, like a mysterious *doppelgänger*, accompanied Khlestakov throughout. His alien presence constituted a mute comment on the progress of the action, when he was not collapsing in a drunken stupor (as in the scene at the mayor's house in Act 3) or playing cards (at the inn in Act 2) with 'Adelaida Ivanovna' – a theme taken straight from *Gamblers*.

The central figure of Khlestakov, played by Erast Garin, appeared strangely garbed and wearing a pair of square, hornrimmed spectacles, looking now like a malignant undertaker, now like a skittish mandarin, next like a pathetic child, in a process of endless transformations. He seemed to constitute the mystery at the heart of the production and at the heart of the play. The presentation became a series of *tours de force*, utilizing the minimal resources of a truck-stage of narrow dimensions which ran on rails from the rear to the front of the stage (in the letter-reading scene in Act 5, for example, and in an invented 'fantasy' scene involving the mayor's wife between Acts 2 and 3). Otherwise, the whole width of the stage was used, on which an arc of polished mahogany doors gleamed as a reflection of the extravagant luxury of an epoch and a location, transferred for Meyerhold's purposes from Gogol's Russian backwoods to a town resembling the capital itself.

The production proved, in many ways, to be a turning-point in Meyerhold's career and still remains one of the most controversial in the history of the Soviet theatre. Critical opinion was divided. The protesters felt that a quasi-mystical element in the character of Khlestakov (especially evident in the famous bribe scene, which Meyerhold staged as a single, universal nightmare rather than as the sequence of scenes laid down in Gogol's text) was incompatible with the clear-sighted rationality of post-revolutionary Soviet society. In some quarters, the production was interpreted as a veiled, semi-subversive comment on the present rather than as a judgement on a period of history which had been overthrown or transcended. Other critics found it difficult to reconcile an apparent stylistic regression, characteristic of his pre-revolutionary work, with the Futurist dynamism of Meyerhold's productions staged during the early 1920s as leader of the 'October in the Theatre' movement.

His defenders included the then Commissar for Education and Enlightenment, Anatoli Lunacharski, as well as his friend, the poet Vladimir Mayakovski. The general public too seemed, on the whole, to be in favour of the production, but more 'official' critics were either scandalized by what they took to be a desecreation of Gogol's

'The Government Inspector'

realistic play, or found a ready target for an incipient hostility felt towards Meyerhold in particular and towards the Russian avant-garde movement in general. The production may be said to have haunted Meyerhold for the rest of his life and provided plenty of ammunition for those who attacked him as a 'formalist' during the 1930s. It still causes difficulties for would-be interpreters as, of course, does the play itself. Nevertheless, Meyerhold's production of *The Government Inspector* is now regarded by theatre historians in both the Soviet Union and elsewhere as one of the remarkable theatrical presentations of the twentieth century.

The initiative for the first performance of the 'canonical' text came from an actor at the Alexandrinski Theatre, P. I. Zubrov, in 1870, and audiences were treated to what, in many respects, seemed a completely different play from the one which had been familiar since 1836. Prior to 1870, it had been conventional to dress the play in contemporary costume – fifties fashion in the 1850s, sixties fashion in the 1860s. In 1870, for the first time, the production was costumed in the style of the 1830s, with corresponding scenery. The director, Yablochkin, had been influenced in this decision by the emergence of so-called 'archeological naturalism' in the European theatre in the 1860s.

Pre-revolutionary productions of *The Government Inspector* tended to become museum pieces, each casting a nostalgically retrospective glance at the past. Even Yablochkin's 1870 version, while it succeeded in breaking away from one tradition, merely managed to establish another which was slavishly imitated by productions which came afterwards. Nineteenth-century stagings of the play were principally memorable for the opportunities with which it presented great actors to interpret fine roles, in particular the roles of the mayor and Khlestakov. As far as interpretations of the mayor are concerned, three main traditions stem from Shchepkin, Sosnitski and Prov Sadovski respectively. Shchepkin emphasized the comic and human aspects of the part and this tendency was brought to perfection by V. N. Davydov. By contrast, Sosnitski played down the comic aspect and did his best not to evoke pity for the mayor. Gogol is said to have preferred Sosnitski's interpretation which, according to the Moscow actor I. V. Samarin, was of a man whose charm was that of a cunning animal into whose clutches some poor victim had fallen. Sadovski's rendering of the mayor was more like a gendarme of the Nicolaevan era than a town official. This tradition was taken up, very successfully, by I. M. Uralov, who acted the part in Stanislavski's 1908 production.

The role of Khlestakov has traditionally presented more difficulties than that of the mayor although, it seems to be generally agreed, the most brilliant individual interpretation of the part has been that of Michael Chekhov in Stanislavski's 1921 production. N. O. Dyur and D. T. Lenski, the first performers, were not very successful. Gogol expressed strong dissatisfaction with Dyur but was quite pleased with S. V. Shumski's version of Khlestakov. Later actors who are said to have succeeded in the part are M. P. Sadovski, who founded a tradition whereby the lying scene was acted in a state of extreme drunkenness, and I. I. Monakhov, who modified this by playing the part as someone who, after a very good meal, became extremely talkative.

The centenary of Gogol's birth was celebrated during the 1908/9 season and was marked by a number of productions of *The Government Inspector*, none more important than that given by Stanislavski at the Moscow Art Theatre. It, too, was conceived in the 'archeologically naturalistic' style of former years and a great deal of time and attention were devoted to achieving an impression of complete authenticity and verisimilitude. Every samovar, teaspoon and ornament was selected to correspond to the 1830s period. An attempt was even made to try and establish the precise town in which the action took place. Khlestakov says he is travelling from Penza to Saratov. The only sizeable town identified on this route was somewhere called Atarsk. A problem arose when it was established by the theatre's research team that Gogol had never been to Atarsk and was unlikely, therefore, to have located the action in this precise place. Eventually, the directors decided to evoke the atmosphere of a town such as the fictitious Mirgorod, where some of Gogol's short stories are set. On the naturalistic level, the production is said to have owed a great deal to the example of the German Saxe-Meiningen company and there were many directorial 'insertions' in the play, such as the scene where Anna Andreyevna orders the room to be prepared for 'the important guest', whereupon an authentically period-piece feather bed was trundled on stage by a whole army of servants.

To describe the overall production as naturalistic is only part of the truth. On this very realistic foundation, Stanislavski constructed an almost abstract version of the play proceeding, as he put it 'from realism outwards, in the direction of the broader and more profound kind of generalization'. The curtain rose on a group of monstrous grotesques who looked as if they had stepped out of the ball scene in Stanislavski's 1907 production of Andreyev's *The Life Of Man*. They moved in slow and stylized fashion, emphasizing their words with strangely sibilant whistles and hisses. Against this background of grotes-querie, the characters of Khlestakov and Osip formed a lively and more human-seeming foreground. A. Goryev, who played Khlestakov acted the part as someone for whom life was just a game. Against a background of the living dead he seemed the only live person, part anti-hero and part clown, despite his somewhat Byronic appearance. The overall impression, according to one critic, was as if observing events on the stage through a giant magnifying glass. The final moments were especially effective as, to the accompaniment of clanking spurs and a heavy tread reminiscent of the statue of the commendatore in Pushkin's *The Stone Guest*, the figure of the gendarme appeared, looking like a gigantic, malignant marionette.[17]

Stanislavski's conception of his 1921 production of *The Government Inspector* also contained the notion of 'the grotesque', which manifested itself 'when content became greater than form'. He wished to stage a phantasmagoria of mass psychosis, in tragi-comic grotesque style, as a whole town came under the spell of the 'petty demon' of a travelling clerk. In order to increase the dynamic of the play's events, Stanislavski contracted the time span to a single day and lit the production accordingly so that, by the time the gendarme arrived at the end, the stage was in almost total darkness. It was in this production that Stanislavski introduced the famous moment when, addressing his remarks to the audience: 'What are you laughing at? You're laughing at yourselves!', he had Ivan Moskvin, who played the mayor, advance to the front of the stage, place one foot on the prompter's box and speak directly out front – this after a whole minute's silence which had been followed by the turning on of the house lights.

However, the production was chiefly memorable for the virtuoso performance of Khlestakov given by Michael

'The Government Inspector'

Chekhov. The tradition which characterized the playing of the part was a well-established one – as superficial dandy and mannered cosmopolitan. Chekhov turned him into a complete nonentity, devoid of any gifts or talent whatsoever, dressed rather childishly in striped trousers. As someone remarked, he acted as if he were a little boy whose favourite pastime was spitting out of a window on to the heads of passers-by, then hiding whilst giving vent to paroxysms of childish delight whenever he scored a hit. Before his confrontation at the inn with the equally terrified but enormous, bear-like figure of Moskvin's mayor, Chekhov, like a frightened child, cowered behind the door whimpering quietly to himself.

The strength of the production, and of Chekhov's performance, was the manner in which this weedy nonentity was transformed into a 'somebody' of terrifying consequence and power – into an image which, according to some, grew to psychopathological proportions. Under the influence of his suddenly acquired grandeur, Chekhov's Khlestakov developed into a being both psychotic and fiendish, while the actor never lost touch with the comic dimension of the performance. One of the moments of transformation has become legendary. It occurred at a point when Chekhov/Khlestakov had been brought back to the mayor's house following lunch at the Charitable Institution. On the rear wall of the reception room hung a full-length uniformed portrait of Tsar Nicholas I in characteristically majestic pose. Chekhov entered the room like a shot from a gun, headed straight for the most dominant point, turned on his heels beneath the portrait of the Tsar and, in a trice, assumed the precise pose and expression of the image behind him.[18] It was an inspired moment which never lost its improvisatory freshness in Chekhov's interpretation and perfectly illustrated the opportunism of the character he portrayed. From now on, it was as if the town officials were in thrall to Khlestakov's improvisatory ability, which rose to greater and greater, more terrifying and more grotesquely comic heights as the lying scene proceeded. Anything became possible for this Khlestakov and every phantasmagorical truth became a potential reality, without any loss of psychological plausibility, under the spell of Chekhov's inspiration. He seemed to be leading a life of mythological proportions in which each of his words and every one of his actions was the potential subject of legend. When describing the 700 rouble melon, this Khlestakov even possessed the amazing confidence to outline a *square* one in the air with his finger, whilst everyone on stage nodded in eager and awestruck recognition. So bold was his performance that, during the wooing scene with the mayor's wife, in a fit of passion, Chekhov even started to clutch and gnaw at a chair leg, then, without in the least destroying the inner coherence of the part, hid in panic under her skirts when he thought he heard the mayor approaching.[19]

Many of the productions of *The Government Inspector* seen in Russia after the Revolution were as scandalously avant-garde as the 1922 production of *Marriage*. The way was led by two versions staged by N. V. Petrov in 1919, the first as 'a play for Red Army men, sailors and workers'. The dominant colour in the setting on each occasion was pink, and the mayor's front parlour had a canary in it as part of an attempt to suggest revolting bourgeois coziness. A production by E. P. Karpov, in 1920, was criticized for mixing the realistic and the grotesque and the curtain fell on the final dumb scene after six seconds. (Gogol asks for a full minute-and-a-half). V. Bebutov's production at the Moscow Trades

'The Government Inspector'

Union Theatre, in 1925, employed constructivist scenery, which could be easily moved to suggest different locations and this was combined with authentic, antiquarian objects, such as table lamps of the period. General anarchy is said to have reigned on stage, where group scenes were played in stylized, grotesque fashion, while other individual roles were acted realistically.

I. Terentyev's 1927 production at the Press House, Leningrad, was described as being constructed according to the principles of 'artistic naturism' (whatever that meant). In what amounted to an eccentric *bouffonade*, actors crawled about the stage and interspersed quotations from Freud and chunks of Polish and Ukrainian among the dialogue. Clutching rolls of toilet paper, each character fought at every other moment to get to a lavatory set in the centre of the stage. The mayor spent most of the play on all fours, explosions were detonated during the course of the action and live mice were released on stage. Costumes were of cubist design with motifs suggestive of each official's trade embroidered on them – a skull on his sleeve for Gibner the doctor, postage stamps and envelopes on the postmaster's trousers. The Charity Commissioner had strawberry designs emblazoned on his rear. (His name, *Zemlyanika*, means 'strawberry')

The production amounted to a scenic interpretation of *The Government Inspector* very much in the Freudian spirit of the critic Ivan Yermakov's interpretation of Gogol's short story *The Nose* which is, more or less, based on the theory that Gogol was a penis fetishist and anal erotic. To the strains of the Moonlight Sonata, Khlestakov went to the toilet clutching a candle. The mayor conducted a whole scene while ensconced on the lavatory, registering his efforts in the tones of his voice. In the wooing scene, Khlestakov disappeared into the lavatory with Marya Antonovna where they were observed by the mayor through the keyhole. The locksmith's wife was taken off behind the divan by Osip, where it soon became obvious that 'relations' were taking place. At the end, the real government inspector turned out to have been Khlestakov all along.[20]

Most productions of *The Government Inspector* seen in England have been adaptations or 'acting versions' which have not always been faithful to the language and meaning of the original, these having been sacrificed as part of an attempt to capture the 'spirit' of the play. In Peter Hall's 1966 production at the Aldwych Theatre, London, this involved setting the play in a remote part of East Anglia and adapting it to fit the rhythms and speech patterns of the local dialect. Paul Scofield acted Khlestakov as a suburban dandy, somewhat past his prime, and Paul Rogers was an astute, countryfied mayor. The costuming throughout tended to emphasize a vaudeville-style approach to the play.

Probably the most successful individual performance was that given by Alec Guinness, who acted Khlestakov in John Burrell's production at the New Theatre, London, in 1948, with settings by Feliks Topolski and with Bernard Miles as the mayor. The adaptation used on this occasion was the one by D. J. Campbell. The major feature of Alec Guinness's portrayal was that it was completely in accord with Gogol's view of the art of comic acting and ran counter to the general tone of the production as a whole which had 'the contours of a charade, like a monstrous balloon'.[21]

The sixties and seventies saw attempts by Henry Livings and Adrian Mitchell to adapt the play for radio and the stage, setting it in an English north country locale and changing names and places accordingly. Oleg Tabakov of the Sovremennik Theatre, Moscow, staged his production of the play, in an English version, at the Crucible Theatre, Sheffield, in 1977 and Toby Robertson directed it at the Old Vic Theatre, London, in 1979 with the Prospect Theatre Company in a production dedicated to Georgi Tovstonogov and influenced by the version which the director had seen at the Gorky Theatre in Leningrad. Here again, the emphasis tended towards vaudeville. Ian Richardson managed to suggest Khlestakov's mindlessness without ever being a source of terrified respect for the town officials, while Barbara Jefford as the mayor's wife acted the part of a Northern vulgarian. The version used on this occasion was the same as for Peter Hall's 1966 production.

Conversation After The Play

Conversation After The Play, or, *Upon Leaving The Theatre After The Performance Of A New Comedy* (to give it its correct title) was written by Gogol in May 1836, shortly after the first performance of *The Government Inspector*. Writing to his friend, N. Ya. Prokopovich, Gogol said that it was written in the heat of the moment and consequently, its attitude towards the figure of the author (Gogol himself) tended to be somewhat immodest. Rather like Molière's *Critique Of The School For Wives*, the play was an answer to Gogol's critics, and many of the points made by the characters refer to actual criticisms of *The Government Inspector* made by specific individuals, such as Bulgarin and Senkovski. Alongside these, Gogol inserted the positive evaluations made by others such as Vyazemski and Androsov. Belinski was wildly enthusiastic about *Conversation After The Play* and noted that it contained a deep appreciation of the theory of social comedy as well as pleasing ripostes 'to all those questions raised by, or rather assaults made on, *The Government*

Inspector and other works by the same author.'[22]

The action of the play or, more strictly, the 'conversation piece', takes place in the foyer of a theatre (presumably the Alexandrinski) after the performance of a controversial comedy (which we take to be *The Government Inspector*). The first to arrive on the scene is the author himself, who has left before the end. He addresses the audience by way of introduction, then conceals himself to hear the verdict of the general public before coming forward again at the end to summarize what he has heard. In between, groups of people leave the auditorium and we, like the author, are privy to their comments in general, which include their remarks on the play. The theatregoers fall into two groups – those who leave at the end of the main play and do not wait for the 'afterpiece' (the latest vaudeville) and those who stay to the very end (the vast majority). The interest of the play is mainly centred on the comments of those who have not stayed to see the vaudeville, many of whom echo Gogol's most cherished views on the theatre and on the nature of comedy in general.

Although Gogol did not write *Conversation* for performance, but rather to be read and pondered over, it was forbidden by the censor because it was thought to contain over-bold judgements on civil servants, the Russian government and the Russian people. It was performed for the first time on the occasion of the fiftieth anniversary of Gogol's death, in 1902, at the Marinski Theatre in St Petersburg.

The First and Second 'Lover of the Arts' express many of Gogol's own ideas on plot and unity of action as well as declaring the right to speak of comedy in the same breath as tragedy. The latter also answers Gogol's critics who declared that the depiction of the base merely panders to baseness:

'The Government Inspector'

Doesn't all this accumulation of base actions, all this miscarriage of law and justice give us a clear idea what law, duty and justice demand of us? In the hands of an expert doctor both cold and hot water can be equally successful in curing the same diseases. In the hands of a man of talent everything can serve as an instrument of the beautiful, provided it is guided by the high ideal to serve the beautiful.

The final word belongs to the author who comes forward from the shadows and pays tribute to the variety of opinions he has heard, both positive and negative, all of these invaluable to a writer. He expresses sadness at the fact that nobody appears to have noticed the existence of the one truly noble character in the play – Laughter – which had the courage to appear despite the low esteem in which it is held. The author enumerates the different qualities of laughter and describes the power of the finest sort, then proceeds to a defence of the despised writer of 'stories'. What was Shakespeare after all but a writer of stories? But what stories! If rejected and misunderstood at the moment, Time, the author feels confident, will put things to rights in sorting out the worthwhile from the worthless and, even if now his position is like that of a weak man as opposed to the proud and the powerful:

> . . . who knows, perhaps it will become universally acknowledged . . . that a proud and powerful man appears to be weak and insignificant in grief and sorrow, while a weak man grows like a Titan amid calamities and, as a result of the same laws . . . he who often sheds deep, heartfelt tears seems to laugh more than anyone in the world.

6
Turgenev's Plays 1834–1848

Turgenev's reputation as a dramatist, in the English-speaking world, rests largely on a single play – *A Month in the Country* – the only one of his plays to be widely available in translation. Yet he was a far more prolific dramatist than Gogol. There are, in fact, five other substantial works which deserve to be considered in the same company: *Where It's Thin, There It Breaks*, *The Parasite*, *The Bachelor*, *Lunch with the Marshal of the Nobility* and *A Provincial Lady* plus two other shorter, but nonetheless interesting works: *Indiscretion* and *Moneyless*. This still does not take into account early works such as *Styeno* and the incomplete *The Temptation of St Antony* or the minor one-act plays *Evening in Sorrento* and *Conversation on the High Road*. In addition to the above, there exist titles and planned outlines of several other plays which were abandoned when Turgenev turned permanently to prose writing. His friend, the poet and editor Nekrasov, thought Turgenev as capable a dramatist as he was a short-story writer and novelist, even going so far as to say that it would be an advantage if he turned his hand permanently to the writing of plays.[1]

His best plays were written in France, mostly during the late 1840s, including *The Parasite*, intended for Shchepkin's benefit but banned on the grounds that it was prejudicial to the good name of the landed gentry. *A Month in the Country*, completed in the early 1850s, was also banned, mainly on moral grounds. Nearly all his plays ran into problems of varying degrees of gravity with the censor, ranging from requests for excision and revision to outright bans on publication and performance. Disheartened by official reaction and by public response to his plays generally, disappointed by indifferent performances of his work in the theatre, Turgenev eventually turned his back on playwriting for good. He revised his existing work from time to time but otherwise turned his attention to the creation of novels and short stories. There is little doubt that he wished to make his mark as a dramatist. It was to drama, after all, that he addressed himself in the first instance. Prose writing had been a secondary attraction. There is also little doubt that Turgenev, like Gogol, although severely limited by the conditions of the theatre of his day, sought to reform the art of theatre and to mould a new form of dramatic writing. Instead he learned, if not exactly to despise the theatre, then seriously to underrate his achievement as a dramatist and, in later years, he was painfully dismissive of work which had cost him dearly in terms of patient creative effort.

Styeno

Literary critics and historians had known of the existence of Turgenev's Romantic drama, *Styeno*, written in the 1830s, but for a long time it was considered lost. It was rediscovered by the Turgenev scholar M. O. Gerzhenson and published in the magazine *Voices Of The Past* in 1913. The adolescent Turgenev began work on the play in September 1834, and completed it in December the same year. It is a substantial work in terms of scale as well as ambition and runs to fifty pages of the 1970 edition of his poems and verse. The handling of the iambic verse form is rather uneven throughout and there are several inconsistencies of scansion (a point which was made to him at the time). Years later, when writing *Rudin*, Turgenev gave some of his own feelings about *Styeno* to the character Lezhnyov:

> You perhaps think I didn't write verses? I did, sir, even a complete drama in the style of *Manfred*. Among the characters there was a ghost with blood on its breast, and not his own blood mark you, but the blood of mankind in general.

In later life, Turgenev admitted to having worshipped Byron in his youth and *Styeno* certainly bears the marks of this idolatry, with many scenes from *Manfred* finding their way into it in barely concealed form.

The Temptation of St Antony

The text of the uncompleted play *The Temptation of St Antony*, about which Turgenev had written to A. A. Bakunin in 1842, was eventually located and published in the *Revue des études slaves,* vol. 30 (1953), by the French scholar André Mazon. Work on the play belongs to the spring of 1842 and the date on the first page of the manuscript is 8 March. In a letter to Bakunin, in early April, Turgenev described how he was 'seeing the play in my sleep'. The first three scenes (the largest) were, he said, complete and there was a character, Annunziata, who, although she was the devil's mistress was, nevertheless, 'an extremely amiable [*prelyubeznaya*] girl etc. etc . . . '.[2] (The word suggests a possible pun on the Russian for 'fornicator' – *prelyubodei*.) At the end of April, Turgenev announced that work on the play was proceeding in fits and starts and mostly by night. That is the last that was heard of it, except for the song which Annunziata sings towards the beginning:

Under the window of the beautiful 'donna'
For more than an hour, in full moonlight
   There walks a youth in love
   Clad in a black velvet cape . .

which appeared in another play, *Two Sisters*, set in Spain, which Turgenev started work on in 1844 and then abandoned. The song took a slightly different form in the second play but what is interesting about both variants is that they prefigure the basic situation in the drama which became *Indiscretion*.

The basis of the rather fantastic plot of Turgenev's *The Temptation of St Antony* was the original legend, but the subject had been suggested to him by Prosper Mérimée's comedy *The Devil Woman*, or *The Temptation of St Antony*; Mérimée had included this in his volume of plays called *The Theatre of Clara Gazul*, which was a hoax in the form of the works of an imaginary Spanish woman playwright, but which had been taken as a kind of French manifesto of Romanticism. Critics had also detected traces of a new realistic direction in the work, which seems to have appealed to Turgenev who, by 1842, had already shed most of his youthful Romantic leanings. The Romantic style in the manner of *Styeno* is both recalled and made fun of in this play, which is in no sense a mere re-working of the Mérimée original but stands as a totally independent work. It parodies the clichés of the saintly life and contrasts realistic scenes set in the boudoir of the courtesan, Annunziata, with romantically fantastic scenes on the seashore, involving devils, imps, clouds and waves (all with speaking parts). In a seemingly complete overthrow of the values enshrined in *Styeno*, Turgenev appears to exalt the real over the ideal and 'exposes over-fervid religious ecstasy'.[3] The experimental aspect of the play is important in so far as it shows Turgenev bent on destroying old forms and reaching forward to a dramatic world which anticipates something akin to Strindberg's *A Dream Play*.

The play, as it exists, occupies twenty pages of the 1970 edition of Turgenev's poems and verse and breaks off part way through Scene 3 at a fairly crucial point in the development. The only substantial gaps are in the 'Chorus Of The Waves', in Scene 3, where Turgenev was clearly having problems with the verse and left some of the lines incomplete. Most of the play is in prose dialogue, except for the songs and choruses. One whole scene of reminiscence between the hermit Antony and his former comrade-in-arms, Carlo Spada, is composed in verse form. The title page describes it as a 'drama in one act'.

Indiscretion

Turgenev's first published dramatic work, like *The Temptation of St Antony*, was a direct result of the influence of Prosper Mérimée's *The Theatre of Clara Gazul*. *Indiscretion,* described as a 'comedy in one act', is a typical product of the Spanish theatre with its serenading under

Turgenev's Plays 1834–1848

balconies, culminating in a bloody drama of jealousy and murder.

The play was first published in 1843 and its only stage production to date was in 1884 when a German company in St Petersburg performed it on two or three occasions in a German version. Belinski recognized a similarity between the 'conversion' of the hero, Victor Alexeyevich (in Turgenev's long poem, *Parasha*) to that of Don Pablo in *Indiscretion*. When Victor marries Parasha he changes from a Byronic hero into a conventional landowner, just as the perpetrator of a *crime passionel*, Don Pablo, metamorphoses into a respectable civil servant in the epilogue to *Indiscretion*. Just as Belinski saw *Parasha* to be 'full of inner content and distinguished by humour and irony', [4] so the parodistic conjunction of ultra-romantic passion with elements of the comedy of manners was seen to characterize *Indiscretion*

One of the interests of the play is that it works in several different modes at once – farcical, romantic and realistic. There seems a clear debt to Molière in the marriage of a young wife to an old husband and in the depiction of the serenading lover who climbs fences and balconies, is threatened by a drunken gardener with a club and a pack of dogs, who hides behind trees to escape detection and, generally, cuts a fairly undignified figure. In the romantic mode there is the crime of passion commited by Don Pablo, as well as elements of Don Rafael's wooing of Donna Dolores. On the realistic level there is an element which can be seen to underlie Mozart's *Don Giovanni*, and which relates to the contemporary position and treatment of women. In this sense, Donna Dolores occupies a position similar to that of Donna Anna and Donna Elvira in the opera. It is probably true to say that, had *Indiscretion* been known to the Feminist Movement, it would not have remained neglected.

Donna Dolores (her name signifies her condition) is twenty-seven and married to a man nearly thirty years her senior. She lives in a house which is guarded like a fortress and which seems to be surrounded by an outer stone wall and an inner picket fence, through which the only access is a gate kept permanently locked and guarded by Pepe, the gardener. Inside the house, Margarita, an old servant, acts as additional guard to Donna Dolores and, when necessary, locks her in her room whenever her husband is away. Dolores has led a permanently sheltered life, having been educated in a convent, and her view of alternatives to her humdrum existence has been gained from romantic novels. It is in this condition, at night on her balcony, that we and the would-be seducer, Don Rafael de-Luna, discover her at the beginning of the play.

The most striking aspect of Donna Dolores is her vulnerability in relation to the predominantly masculine world around her. To Don Rafael she is an innocent fool to be sexually exploited. To her husband (until his feelings of security are undermined) she is an object of consumption, or a fetishist plaything. For Don Pablo Sangre (whose name suggests his bloodiness) she serves as the focus of all his frustrated passions which exist irrespective of their object and which can just as easily turn to mad destructiveness. Even for Margarita, she is the personification of all her class frustrations in a world where the servant sees 'riches' as of prime importance. She even blames the innocent Donna Dolores for the evil effects of such values on her own daughter. The actual causes of both their sufferings are shown to be the men who control their lives and the male-dominated society which exists to perpetuate these forms of control. The metaphor used to describe the relationship between the male characters in the play and Donna Dolores is that of cat to mouse. Don Balthasar d'Esturiz says, as he contemplates the prospect of Donna Dolores awaiting his return:

> I remember, when a good juicy, ripe pear was given to me, I did not eat it right away like any other foolish boy or scapegrace . . . no, I would sit down, stealthily take the pear out of my pocket, examine it from all sides, kiss it, stroke it, put it to my lips, take it away again – admire it from a distance, admire it close to, then, at last, shut my eyes and bite into it. Ah, I really should have been born a cat.

Later, when Don Pablo is contemplating murder, he describes Donna Dolores as being 'in his claws' and there is a sense in which Don Rafael's playful asides to the audience, as he comments on the naïveté of his victim, also convey a predatory aspect to the seduction.

The men in the play are revealed as inferior, passionately, to Donna Dolores. The double fence which surrounds her is more a barrier to their own male fear of passion than it is a bar to female feeling. The 'weak spot' in the barrier, which has to be built higher and stronger, refers more to their own incarceration in a prison of suppressed emotion than it does to the suppression of women. (Turgenev uses this image of a barrier, or dam, built against the release of emotion in *Where It's Thin, There It Breaks* and also in *A Month in the Country*.) Don Pablo's love, which has turned to destructive hate, appears as a direct product of this involuted self-suppression.

The final scene of the play contains the confrontation between the insane Don Pablo and Donna Dolores. He confesses his love and recognizes that she has nothing but contempt for him. The intention to murder her has been there from the outset and the prolongation of the scene becomes a form of perverse luxury. When faced with death, Donna Dolores, who has been conscious of a sense of fate, is superbly and pathetically defiant. A final irony is her declaration of love for the pitiful Don Rafael. In a denouement reminiscent of Lessing's *Emilia Galotti*, the male murderer stands holding the knife over the murdered female but here the real tragedy is obscured by the selfconscious melodramatization of the male protagonists, who experience the situation as an illustration of their own tragic destiny, in a manner which anticipates Ibsen. An epilogue of a few lines, depicting the scene ten years later, sets the seal on the 'comedy':

> *Scene: The Office of an important official. A secretary at the table. Enter Don Pablo Sangre, Count of Torreno.*
> COUNT PABLO: (*busily to the secretary*) Are my papers ready? It's time for me to . . . .
> SECRETARY: (*respectfully*) Here they are, your Highness. (*Both go out*).

Not only has the murder gone unpunished but Don Pablo appears to have been elevated to the rank of Count. Aristocratic and bureaucratic life goes on over the corpses of the victims. Commenting on this façade, Don Pablo had earlier remarked:

> True, some eccentric person might think a crime was being committed in the house, or was about to be committed . . . . But that's all nonsense. Here are living modest, quiet, settled people . . . .

Turgenev's Plays 1834–1848

Moneyless

Nothing appears more surprising than Turgenev's decision in 1845, following the composition of *Indiscretion*, to turn his attention to a pure Russian vaudeville. The main influence in his attempt to exploit a debased genre appears to have been the example of Gogol, especially in the choice of milieu and in the conception of the central characters, Zhazikov and Matvyei. Another influence can be seen in the increasing popularity, during the 1840s in Russia, of vignettes of Russian life in prose form, in which the manners and mores of specific classes were depicted with considerable fidelity – the so-called 'physiological sketches' of the Natural School which Russian criticism refers to, and which find a counterpart in the pictorial art of the period. In *Moneyless*, however, Turgenev exploits vaudeville only superficially; the play is devoid of the traditional couplets, the conventional love intrigue and only retains one typical device – the string of creditors who call at Zhazikov's apartment, but here each is a carefully delineated social type, not a caricatural mask.

The Russian title *Bezdenezh'e* literally means 'one without money' and the play is, indeed, about money and the lack of it. At the same time, it is like a kaleidoscope through which can be observed the changing patterns of a whole social system. Through the close-up technique of the vaudeville-cum-physiological sketch, Turgenev offers a view of a complete social process and a changing society. The play's subtitle is *Scenes From The Petersburg Life Of A Young Nobleman*. The young nobleman (clearly modelled on Khlestakov) and his servant (very like Osip) occupy an apartment on an upper (that is, inferior) floor of a St Petersburg tenement house. The life-style of the young man is at odds with his claim to the title of nobleman. He is penniless and the apartment is modest. During the course of the action various representatives of the emerging class of city tradesmen, the petty bourgeoisie, call on him virtually non-stop in an attempt to retrieve debts, while the master feigns absence and leaves his servant to deal with the callers. Finally, an acquaintance from the country appears, who lends him some money, and the play ends with a comment from the servant on how times have changed.

At the centre of the play is Zhazikov. He has left his family estate in the country in charge of his ageing mother and has settled in St Petersburg, the centre of everything epitomizing the truly noble existence in early nineteenth-century Russia. The implication is that the estate is rapidly deteriorating, while Zhazikov squanders family money. He appears to represent the culmination of a process of profligacy and waste, but acts as if no change at all were taking place and the status of the nobility unaffected; as if this concept were in some miraculous fashion separable from the possession of money. The play sets out to demonstrate the vacuousness of the notion of 'the nobleman' once the basis of superiority, in the form of property and wealth, is absent. Zhazikov and Matvyei retain and act out their roles as master and servant in circumstances which are ludicrously inappropriate, and yet their identities depend entirely on this notion of role-playing. The actual reversal of these roles, with the pattern of their necessary maintenance for the parties concerned, is conveyed with superb comic effect. Whenever a creditor calls, this is accompanied by the persistent ringing of a bell. The aristocrat (the conventional ringer of the bell to summon a servant) starts like a frightened hare on each occasion and runs for cover. It has become an almost Pavlovian motif by the end of the play as we observe the nobleman reduced to his reflexes. Meanwhile, Matvyei assumes the role of the master in confronting the creditors, as well as becoming the spokesman for aristocratic values.

The comedy of the piece is skilfully contrived and is mainly based on contradictions and contrasts within what is said and between the various characters who come and go, three of whom are never seen by the audience. Turgenev makes great play with the spectator's imaginative capacity to envisage the character behind the highly flavoured speech patterns and is particularly successful in the case of the invisible merchant – anxious about his money and constantly returning to the topic with mechanical variations on the same phrase: 'There's none lying around by any chance?', and torn between not wishing to appear presumptuous or over-pressing and a natural impulse to lay his hands on what is owed him.

The arrival of Blinov, the acquaintance from the country, highlights a principal social theme of the play – the contrast, but at the same time the fundamental connection, between town and country. The country, for Matvyei the servant, represents tradition and a secure master and serf relationship whose lineage he describes in the family as he remembers it in Zhazikov's grandfather's and in his father's time. 'Things are not what they used to be', says Matvyei; 'Your grandfather, Timofei Lukich, blessed be his memory, was a very tall man', he declares, as if the present were composed of midgets. In fact, the terms of Matvyei's description of the members of the family are reminiscent of the decaying grotesques who populate Gogol's *Dead Souls*. Zhazikov, by contrast, has nothing but contempt for the country, where he sees 'lack of education' and unattractive girls. An ironic point here is that his range of choice in St Petersburg appears to extend all the way from one 'Verochka' to the laundry girl who calls with a bill. Matvyei wants to be a serf, and a serf is not a serf in town. Zhazikov wants to be an aristocrat – and how can one be an aristocrat in the country?

In an extended soliloquy, Zhazikov eventually manages to convince himself that things are not so bad in the country after all – a recognition of the need to return and try to get the estate into some sort of order. But the contemplated return becomes a nostalgic turning-back of the clock, as if the process of superannuation, so obviously present in the context of the city, did not extend to include the landed estates which were now rapidly being engrossed by a new entrepreneurial class with business acumen.

Blinov represents the new type. His description of the prolonged legal wrangling about estate boundaries, which he is disputing with his neighbour, and which he has come to the capital to settle in court, suggests just how closely the apparent opposites of town and country are linked. We also gain an insight into what St Petersburg actually represents for Zhazikov. He shares Blinov's eagerness to combine going to the theatre to see 'a tragedy' with dining out at 'a cafe with an organ' and visiting the circus to watch big fat 'mamzelles' who 'ride standing on horses'. There is an element of condescension in Zhazikov's expression of his willingness to introduce Blinov to these delights, but they appear to represent to him the apotheosis of city culture.

The play ends with Zhazikov and Blinov going off to the tragedy and to the circus. Now that he has been lent some money, the country can 'go to the devil'. Matvyei concludes the action with an ultra-conservative remark addressed at the back of the departing Blinov, whom he recognises as the new breed of master:

Turgenev's Plays 1834–1848

Gone is the Golden Age! How changed is the nobility!

Where It's Thin, There It Breaks

In 1847, Turgenev attended a performance of Alfred de Musset's 'proverbe', *Un Caprice* in Paris. The dramatic form of the 'proverbe' was originally that of a charade designed to illustrate the proverbial saying which formed the last line of the play and it was this form which Turgenev adopted for his next comedy, written in 1848, for the St Petersburg actress V. V. Samoilova. The work is conceived in an altogether different style from his previous plays. The emphasis is on the subtle psychological interplay of feeling which underlies the surface of salon-play dialogue. A more genuine level of reality surfaces when the flimsy veil ruptures at its most vulnerable points.

Musset's theatre was very popular in Russia at the time and continued to be so. Later, Tchaikovsky is said to have been wildly enthusiastic about his work. Even plays which were not popular in Paris were highly successful in St Petersburg and, in fact, the triumphant de Musset revival at the Comédie Française, which really began with the production of *Un Caprice* witnessed by Turgenev, owed much to the championing of his cause by the Russian actress A. M. Karatygina.

Where It's Thin, There It Breaks depicts the attempts of Vera Nikolayevna, the daughter of a rich landowning widow, Anna Vasilyevna Libanova, to get Gorski, the son of a female neighbour, to marry her. The action is set against the background of the Libanova country house, a resplendent eighteenth-century edifice of Italian design in the Russian countryside. Vera's romantic view of love and marriage is opposed by Gorski's more cynical realism, and the plot concerns the latter's emotional vacillation – first romantically susceptible and then prosaically disinclined. The action climaxes in Vera's frustrated acceptance of the proposal of the naïve and lovesick Stanitsyn, an action which contains, as part of its intention, an attempt to pierce the protective shell of Gorski's egotism. In the background hover a third suitor, Mukhin, the governess Mlle Bienaimé, a Captain Chukhanov, who is a permanent guest in the Libanova household, and Libanova's companion and relation, Varvara Ivanovna.

The play's first performance was given on 10 December 1851, and was not a success. It was revived at the Alexandrinski Theatre in 1891 and, more successfully, at the Moscow Art Theatre in 1912, with Olga Knipper and Vasili Kachalov. Kachalov acted Gorski as someone whose ideas and desires are weakened by coldness of spirit, exhausted by egotism and fruitless activity of the mind. This view of the character corresponds to a tendency in Russian criticism to see Gorski as one of the first dramatic embodiments of the 'superfluous man'. Typically, he is a scion of the upper class, cut-off intellectually from that class and from society as a whole, doomed to agonize self-obsessively over every action and to sully everything of worth with which he comes into contact, either from a sense of world-weary cynicism or in a spirit of casual destructiveness. The prototype of the species is considered to be Pushkin's Eugene Onegin. Turgenev wrote his own *Diary of a Superfluous Man* in 1850 and the type is well described by Alexander Herzen:

> The distinguishing feature of our epoch is *grübeln* [to deliberate]. We do not wish to take a step without first having thought about it; we constantly delay, like Hamlet, and think, think. . . . There is no time to act; we chew interminably over both the past and the

present, everything which is happening to us and to others; we seek justification, clarification, enquire into ideas and truths.[5]

The play can be described as Turgenev's version of Gogol's *Marriage*. At one point Gorski declares that he will not, like Podkolyosin, leap out of the window but will leave quietly by the door into the garden. The irony is that he sees this as superior behaviour when, in fact, Turgenev implies that the leap from the window had something to recommend it. It was at least unconventional. Everyone in the play is in the grip of convention. Everything is codified by rules and regulations. The characters appear to be trapped between two worlds – the world of Nature on the one hand and the world of art and artifice on the other, between romantic ideals and prosaic realities. The only way in which they chart a course between the 'Scylla' of the one and 'Charybdis' of the other (to borrow Gorski's mythological terminology) is through the establishment of civilized rules and conventions. But these merely succeed in parodying the 'higher', more spiritual, sides of the equation while suppressing the connection with the 'lower', more prosaic and physical sides of reality – an aspect of severance from the natural world in general. The characters exist in a kind of limbo, part flesh, part spirit, struggling half-heartedly towards a higher unity of opposites. As in Gogol's play, the symbol of that desired unity is marriage, seen by some as an end in itself, recognized by others as an evasion. Ideal marriage involves the unity of opposites. Actual marriage is a ritualized and conventionalized hollow unity masking an essential separateness.

Critics usually see Vera as in some sense superior to Gorski – she a kind of Don Quixote, he a Hamlet figure. The truth, however, is that Vera's positive, almost

Shavian, drive towards improving the species through marriage with Gorski is revealed as a parodied version of natural and instinctive drives, just as his retreat into the world of the mind in order to counter her assault on his emotions is revealed as a parodied version of the world of intellect and imagination. Both are entirely conventional creatures whose egos just happen to be more strongly developed than others. The desirable conflict, leading to a unity of opposites, is presented as a petty egotistical affair which, instead of leading to a synthesis on a higher plane, leads to a false unity on a lower plane – the marriage between Vera and Stanitsyn.

As well as being a very Gogolian play, we are reminded of Turgenev's interest in the Hegelian dialectic but, in this instance, the conflicts are presented in all their hollowness. There is much talk of winning and losing, which metaphorically links the world of human action with talk of military conflict and with game-playing. Losing and winning have become the human by-products of a petty and meaningless conflict. The recognition of the necessity of battle is implicit within the play, but winning or losing in a conventional sense is shown not to be the point. For the most part, the characters evade the recognition of necessary struggle, or take part in activities which merely parody it. They view life in a petty, individualistic way where there can only be the see-saw oppositions between 'higher' and 'lower', 'winner' and 'loser'. Never, it seems, can the conflict be converted into a higher synthesis through concerted human struggle. The 'break' in the play occurs at the thinnest point between opposites – between winning and losing, between male and female, between the ideal and the real, between art and nature. It is as if the fabric of life were being tugged from opposed ends, destructively, instead of being co-operatively woven into clearer and more durable form. Because there exists no co-ordinated and conscious recognition of the pattern and purpose of struggle, its parodied version takes the form of the love duel and games of chance, where there is opposition but no genuine conflict and the outcome is based on arbitrariness and hazard.

There are two symbolic gestures in the play which appear as intended parallels. Vera plucks a rose to give to Gorski but is then prevented from doing so by the presence of Mukhin. She ends by throwing aside the rose, which Gorski later picks up and puts in his pocket. The parallel is with the action of Captain Chukhanov. He is kept on sufferance in the Libanova household as a permanent guest and to make up a third at card games. He has been picking mushrooms in the garden, which he then offers to Libanova in his hat. Her response is to tell him that a hat is no place for mushrooms; they belong on a plate. The mushrooms have been stooped for at ground level, are then placed in something taken from the head and, in this form, are offered in a gesture of self-effacing generosity. The only dialectic appreciated by Libanova is a connection between mushrooms and plates as an aspect of conventional propriety. Although only a modest moment of synthesis, the significance of Chukhanov's gesture evades her consciousness entirely. Turgenev intends that it should not escape us. By contrast, the rose is offered in a totally different spirit. Vera intends it as a symbol, which implicates her feelings for Gorski and his for her. The presence of Mukhin forces her to lie and say that she picked it for herself. But the lie contains a truth. She did, in fact, pick it for herself, because she is symbolized by it and projects her own feelings into the rose as symbol. It is a gesture of pure egotism. Once its extraneous value is redundant, she casts the rose aside and the original plucking of the flower can now be seen as a wilfully destructive action. Gorski's placing it in his pocket merely compounds the desecration. He will produce the rose at the end of the play, wilted, merely in order to humiliate Vera with a reminder of the evanescence of her feelings for him.

The figure of the captain is allied with that of the companion, Varvara Stepanovna. They are the dialectical opposites of Gorski and Vera but occupy an equivalent position of importance in the play. Varvara Stepanovna appears to count hardly at all in the scheme of things, like Ivanov in *The Parasite*. She and the captain say very little but, in the triangular card game, it is she who appears to deliberately 'lose' in order that the captain should 'win'. Their saying nothing, or next to nothing, becomes the dialectical opposite of the pointless garrulousness of the protagonists. Their possessing nothing is the opposite of the others' possessing everything. They emerge, strangely, as the hero and heroine of the play, linking arms in military formation at the end when the group prepares to march 'out there', into the forest. The two are linked together by the notion of service. The captain's final words are 'Ready to serve'. Excursions into the outer world appear brief and hazardous. The captain, like Zhevakin in *Marriage*, has made these sorties and knows what it is to 'storm a fortress' – a version of the eternal conflict which has its own lessons to teach about the capacity of humans for violence and suffering. The others venture out timidly in the rain and sun and have to scurry back to the protective confines of their Rastrellian dwelling. What could better exemplify the absurd challenge which one form of art lays before nature than the erection of a Rastrellian mansion in the wilderness of the Russian countryside? The more permanent forms of challenge, or transcendence, are made by poetry and music, the first of which Gorski despises, the second of which Vera merely dabbles in.

Poetry appears to occupy an equivalent position in this play to the rose plucked by Vera. It is only seen to exist as an appendage of the egos of the characters. The most poetic moment is the evocation, by Gorski, of the moonlit night on the lake where he has rowed Vera Nikolayevna and when, as he describes it, he almost lost control of himself under the spell of her physical proximity and the moonlit setting, even going to the lengths of delivering himself of some verses by Lermontov. The first thing to note is that Gorski's recounting of this magical moment is in a mood of cynical disavowal and shame, now that the spell has worn off. It is also a betrayal of Vera's confidence, which he calculates Mukhin will relay to her and so precipitate the untying of the emotional knot he fears has been made by the shared experience. What we also note is another kind of betrayal in the egotistically false note of the poetic evocation. Nature is reduced to a mere theatrical backdrop for the posings of the characters. The lake becomes reduced to a modest-sized pond and the light on the scene comes as much from the candle held by the watchful Mlle Bienaimé on the balcony as it does from any actual moon.

The musical moment comes later, when the two egos of Vera and Gorski clash, again under the watchful eye of Mlle Bienaimé, as Vera accompanies herself on the piano (a Clementi sonata) while carrying on an accusatory conversation with Gorski. The beauty of the music is incidental to her self-expression and she even uses the music, in the manner of the rose, to add symbolic emphasis to what she is saying by 'beating hard on the keys' or 'playing gently' when she is being more seductive. The comic irony here is that she seems to be a merely average dilettante. The tête-à-tête is interrupted by Mlle Bienaimé's dry cough and her pointed remark that the sonata 'sounds difficult to play'.

Gorski turns out to be contemptuous of poetry and poetic natures: 'Long live mockery, hilarity and malice', he declares, 'Now I am again in my element'. (The phrase he uses translates literally as 'on my own plate again' – a conscious echo of the earlier episode with the mushrooms.) In opting out of marriage, he has opted out of the dialectic into singleness and has thrown away the poetic part of himself, just as earlier he had cast aside the novel he was reading, the contents of which seemed to him to be just obvious foolishness. He can only joke at the end of the play. *'Welche Perle warf ich weg!'* (What a pearl I've thrown away!) – the retreat into a foreign language being part of the evasion. He has also thrown the more precious part of himself away but can only melodramatize his situation – the gall and bile which rise in his throat being the consequence of egotistically wounded pride where Vera's sword-thrust (her engagement to Stanitsyn) can be seen to have found its mark. Words are the only protection he has against his own nullity, which he chooses to think of as complexity: 'Don't tear the last decisive word out of me . . .' he begs Vera as he dodges this way and that to escape definition, because in his heart of hearts he suspects that in veering between one state and another he has ended up as nothing.

Gorski is very fond of attributing everything to Fate or Chance and wondering whether Fate is laughing at him or assisting him. He plays a game on his own whereby the chance potting of a billiard ball will be seen to determine his fate. Recognizing this as mere childishness, he throws the cue aside. Yet the tripartite pattern of the game itself is important, although Gorski does not recognize the fact. He has earlier said in conversation with Mukhin that his task was to chart a course between Scylla and Charybdis. The point becomes the active charting of a course and not the leaving of matters to chance, just as the skill in billiards involves a relationship between three elements and maintaining those elements in play.

What, finally, is the implication of the proverb which forms the title to the play? What does Mukhin mean when he quotes it at the end? He would seem to be referring to a 'break' in Gorski's ego which his manifestation of high spirits is not quite managing to disguise. Anyone who attempts to exist through mere singularity (and all are single in this play) construct the world purely in terms of the self, the most extreme manifestation of which is egotism. The finale produces the harnessing of couples – a realignment of forces within a group – for the march to the forest. However, allying yourself to another, or forming ranks, does not automatically overcome the problem, but can constitute other kinds of weakness, or thinness. The relationship between Vera and Stanitsyn seems especially vulnerable. Between the captain and Varvara Ivanovna there is a kind of unity of relationship, although not a particularly profound one, which is synthesized in a third element – that of 'service'. Anna Vasilyevna simply represents indomitable egotism and it is apt that she joins ranks with Gorski in the finale. The case of Mlle Bienaimé appears to be slightly different. She is not just a governess and watchdog but has something of the spiritual guardian about her as both worker and educator. The most striking images of her presence in the play are when she is seen holding a candle on the balcony, providing a third element in this moment of epiphany, this Moonlight Sonata, and also, when she sits, working a pattern on canvas, during the piano-playing scene. She appears to be a comic version of a dialectical trinity, the three in one, offering work, service and enlightenment. One of her final actions, in order to 'win' Mukhin, is to engage him in a game of billiards which she 'loses' (we suspect that she ensures that he wins).

As well as the debt to de Musset, we are reminded of how steeped in the work of Shakespeare Turgenev had been since childhood. The subtitle of this, his most Shakespearian, as well as his most de Musset-like play, might well be *Much Ado About A Midsummer Night's Dream of Nothing*.

7
Turgenev's Plays 1848–1850

The Parasite

Turgenev's second major play for the professional theatre, *The Parasite*, was written at the request of Shchepkin and completed, in France, in 1848. Like the pictures in the album which Mukhin contemplates in *Where It's Thin, There It Breaks* of 'views from Italy' – with the suggestion of a reciprocal process, both 'views of' and 'views from' – this play is a view of Russia 'from abroad', where one of the characters, Tropachov, always intends going but, instead, has to make do with lithographs in an album. The play was immediately banned, ostensibly because, according to the censor, it presented the Russian nobility in a 'contemptuous light'.

The Parasite circulated in manuscript and achieved quite wide popularity. It was first published in *The Contemporary*, in 1857, under the title *Alien Bread* and the first performance was permitted in 1861. During the nineteenth century and, occasionally since, the two-act play has been presented as a one-acter, leaving out the whole of the second part and concluding with the revelation of Kuzovkin's paternity at the end of Act 1. The actor V. N. Davydov was among the first to appreciate what a travesty this was when he wrote:

> I cannot understand how Russian actors have not been able, and are still unable, to understand the beauty of the second act, finding it faded and pale, even unnecessary. The second act is unconditionally stronger and more artistic than the first. It is full of incomparable psychology.[1]

The parasite in question is Vasili Semyonich Kuzovkin, who has lived on the estate of the Korin family for the past thirty years, fourteen of which have been spent in the company of the daughter of the deceased owners and an aunt who looked after the girl following the death of her mother. Olga Petrovna, the daughter, moved to St Petersburg at the age of fourteen and is now returning to her family estate seven years later in the company of her newly acquired husband, a thirty-two-year-old, town-bred collegiate councillor, Pavel Nikolayevich Yeletski. Kuzovkin still lives on the estate, which continues to be staffed by a retinue of servants, because of a prolonged legal wrangle surrounding the settlement of his own inherited property which has gone on for the past twenty years or so. In Korin's time, Kuzovkin appears to have served as a butt for the cruel humour of a tyrannical master who, as well as being consistently unfaithful to his wife, was an unpredictable and violent man. The memory of Kuzovkin's role as 'estate fool' is revived by the arrival of an old friend of the family, the neighbour Tropachov, who has come to greet the newly-weds. In a scene reminiscent of

Turgenev's Plays 1848–1850

baited into recounting the history of his abortive litigation, mocked at and, finally, crowned with a fool's cap. His response to this revival of earlier humiliations is to declare in the presence of the young husband, and within earshot of the daughter, that he is, in fact, her real father.

The second act deals with the aftermath of this revelation, in which Kuzovkin first declares this admission to have been madness and then, in private conversation with Olga, says it is true. Out of a sense of loyalty to her husband, Olga conveys this to him. He, in turn, seeks to remove Kuzovkin from the house by buying his confession to having told a lie, giving him enough money to purchase his estate from in chancery and over the head of rival claimants – the heirs of a German called Hanginmester. Olga eventually persuades Kuzovkin to accept the money, and his departure is explained by the announcement that he has finally 'come into his estate'. He leaves, having reached an agreement in confidence to have private conference with 'his daughter' whenever he should visit the Yeletski estate in future.

The first production opened on 30 January 1862, at the Bolshoi Theatre, Moscow, for Shchepkin's benefit performance and with a strong cast. The play was revived at the Alexandrinski Theatre in 1889 for V. N. Davydov's benefit, when only the first act was presented, then again in 1916 when it was acted in its entirety. The first act was given as part of the Moscow Art Theatre's *Turgenev Evening*, in 1912. Just before his death, Davydov revived his performance as Kuzovkin during the 1924–25 season at the Maly Theatre, Moscow. In an otherwise lukewarm review in *Pravda*, the critic Pavel Markov described Davydov's performance as:

. . . material for research not only into the art of the

actor, but into the lives of the insulted and the injured such as Davydov shows us in the parasite Kuzovkin.[2]

The reference to the 'insulted and injured' is a common one in Russian criticism of the play which places it, as Marc Slonim has pointed out, in a line which 'stems from Gogol's "little man", later taken up by Dostoevski',[3] with Akaki Akakyevich, in *The Overcoat*, as a forerunner.

Davydov was right when he pointed to the wealth of psychological matter in the play. At the same time, most critics would seem to be wrong in regarding it as a defence of the 'little man', in addition to its being a criticism of feudal Russia. English translators tend to evade a recognition in the play's title, *Nakhlebnik*, of a direct meaning of 'parasite' in favour of the more neutral 'The Boarder', 'A Poor Gentleman', or 'The Family Charge'. Foreign translations opt for the even more neutral *Alien Bread*. However, the true significance of the play needs to be seen to depend upon the recognition that the meanings of *nakhlebnik* are negative. It *is* a Gogolian play, but its roots lie less in *The Overcoat*, as is generally thought, than in the Gogol work which Tropachov refers to indirectly in Act 2 when he speaks of the Emperor or China, namely *The Diary of a Madman*. Seen in this light, the play becomes an altogether different and more original, as well as more profound, artistic work.

The themes of the play can be stated, in general terms, as social breakdown and fragmentation accompanied by loss of meaning and individual identity. The loss of connection in the social world is paralleled in the more intimate world of personal and family relationships. People move and respond to the dictates of natural instinct and appetite, or to the mechanical and tyrannical demands of convention and habit, or out of a grossly distorted sense of their own individual significance – an aspect of an attempt to counter the prevailing sense of a loss of individual meaning. In this situation, those at the bottom of the heap serve to confirm the identity of those at the top. A psychological means of asserting one's own value is to imagine oneself, like Gogol's madman, to be the Emperor of China. Those at the top of the heap can only tolerate this destabilization of hierarchical order by describing the claim as mad. To a certain extent, this is what happens when Kuzovkin makes a claim for his own worth, by asserting a consanguinous relationship with the wife of a 'high Petersburg official'. The complication arises from the fact that, whereas we recognise Poprishchin's claim to be the Emperor of China as 'false', there are less good reasons for doubting Kuzovkin's claim to be Olga's father. Yet, the situation which Turgenev portrays is a form of madness. The division between social and personal worlds is given poignant significance through the *making public* of the claim. To 'go out of one's mind', in this sense, is to make generally public knowledge that which was hitherto personally intimate. The reason Kuzovkin 'goes out of his mind', lies in the fact that the claim to paternity has less to do with the fact of intimate feeling and blood relationship, than with his claim for his own *individual* significance in *this kind of world*. In brilliant fashion, Turgenev dramatizes the claim for, and the attribution of, identity of an inherently false kind, as well as the simultaneous destruction of true identity in the human connection between father and daughter. To declare that Kuzovkin *is* mad, as he frequently describes himself to be, and as he is frequently described by others, flies in the face of generally accepted readings of the play, but madness, social and personal, appears to be its crucial theme.

The opening is almost pure 'theatre of the grotesque' and owes much to Gogol's fragment *The Servants' Hall*. Presided over by the grotesque *maitre d'hotel*, Trembinski, who is given the physical attributes of a puppet and whose personal existence is merely instrumental to the requirements of a sanctioned hierarchy, the contemporary life of the estate moves to the mechanized rhythms of his motorized responses, seen in contrast to the patterns and rhythms of the past compounded of chaos and inertia. The superficial contrast is between the values of the town and those of the country, between the new values and the old – Trembinski insisting on a strict, mechanized division of labour and organization for their own sake, where the estate managers have been content to let matters go to rack and ruin while lining their own pockets in the absence of authority. The contrast between town and country is intensified by the arrival of the 'new man', the Petersburg councillor Yeletski, the new estate owner, for whom the language of estate management might just as well be Chinese. He too moves in the mechanical grooves carved out by utilitarian principles, conventional procedures and the dictates of social propriety, while emanating the mystifying aura of authority which attaches to his quasi-aristocratic background and his hailing from St Petersburg.

Identity becomes a matter of passive submission to a preordained social role, whether that of servant or master, and yet there persist the claims for individual meaning and significance. Turgenev makes great play with people's names, a normal aspect of identity which is here thrown into disarray. 'Who are you?' Trembinski asks the baffled Pyotr and when the latter offers his name is told that his true identity is 'lackey'. The attempt to identify throughout is not to discover an authentic individuality, but to place in a social scale of higher and lower. This is especially true of the men. They deliberately forget each other's names, or get the right first name and the wrong patronymic as part of the pattern of social and self-assertion. All that appears to matter is the pecking order, while human connection is lost in the process. Humanity is commonly seen as being reasserted in the human claims voiced by Kuzovkin, but these are, in fact, part of that same process. A vestigial humanity persists only on the margins – in the person of the young servant, Masha, who laughs at the absurd ritual which welcomes the newly-weds; in Kuzovkin's friend, Ivanov, who is a passive, almost silent witness to the underlying truth; and in Olga Petrovna herself, who is torn apart, finally, by her attempt to reconcile the claims of society, represented by her husband, and the claims of her nature, represented by her daughterhood.

The central character, Kuzovkin, exemplifies the schizophrenic nature of the society and embodies the split within himself. He is both the most self-effacing and the most self-assertive person in the play. He is at the bottom of the social heap, yet possesses the conventionally superior feelings of a nobleman. He is both the most inarticulate and the most rhetorical, the most self-important and the most self-demeaning. His existence is a surrogate existence. He is, in fact, a parasite. Kuzovkin is an integral part of the grotesque elements in the play; his habits of mind are entirely conventional and completely mechanical. His account of the legal proceedings surrounding the inheritance of his estate is presented in a manner which, ironically, justifies the 'cruel' laughter with which it is received. It is manic in its obsessiveness and in its command of intricate detail, as well as giving the impression of mechanical repetitiveness – in the recurrence of the word *veksel* (a bill of exchange), for example, and in the exhausted repetitions at the end of the long speech towards the end of Act 1 as the machine of his mind winds down. The process of litigation is relayed as a form of madness, a metaphor of breakdown, setting individual members of the same family against each other while dividing the estate 'to the fourteenth part'. The final attribution of blame to the ubiquitous 'Hanginmester', Turgenev asks us to note, actually represents the mechanical principle itself, as Kuzovkin wrestles with his name: 'Han-han-han-gin-mester'.

The irony of this pathetic scene, which culminates in the fool's cap being set on Kuzovkin's head, is that it is simultaneously his humiliation *and* his moment of glory. Being humiliated is an essential aspect of his identity. It is essential to his ultimate feeling of superiority to those who humiliate him. It provides him with opportunities for self-assertion as when, previously, he fathered the illegitimate child and, now, announces the fact. These scenes of abasement are the only moments in his life when his essentially selfconscious and theatrical personality finds itself at the centre of the stage, the focus of attention. This craving for attention might be explicable, even tolerable, in a disturbed child. In a fifty-year-old adult the signs are ominous. It is inevitable that the demand for social recognition cannot satisfy the claims of personal identity. These can only be harboured in the mind, as ideals. Once released into the light of day, the one claim cancels the other. The truth and reality of the father/daughter relationship can only be sustained as an ideal of the mind. Once it becomes instrumental in the claim for social recognition, its inherent quality is destroyed at the moment of its public utterance. Kuzovkin is, indeed, mad to have 'come out of his mind'. The accompanying stage

Turgenev's Plays 1848–1850

direction is 'Olga disappears'. Yeletski's conventional recognition – 'You're mad' – veils a perception at a deeper and more tragic level of this apparent comedy.

As usual, in Turgenev, the victim is a woman. Olga only exists to serve her husband's interests or as an aspect of Kuzovkin's identity. She is neither true wife nor true daughter. She is a victim of this instrumentality just as her dead mother was a victim of her husband's brutality. Olga is further humiliated by her husband in being made instrumental in buying off Kuzovkin. The latter will not accept the 10,000 roubles from Yeletski out of a sense of his dignity as a nobleman (a way of seeking a moral advantage over his ostensible 'superior'). Olga agrees to act as her husband's emissary in a tactical sense, and acknowledge her daughterhood, in order to force Kuzovkin to accept the money. In a brilliant dramatic stroke, Turgenev has Kuzovkin first drop the paper-bill and then accept it when it is physically pressed on him by Olga, who simultaneously says she believes him to be her father. At the point of genuine human contact, the promissory note comes between. The revelation of natural connection involves a simultaneous cancellation of that connection. Olga's recognition of Kuzovkin as a father *in these terms* actually severs her connection with him as a daughter. Because the acceptance of the money sanctions a social lie for propriety's sake, it also makes a lie of the personal relationship. The agreement to carry on an illicit, secret sense of their true kinship, under the umbrella of the social life, becomes both ironic and pathetic. It can possibly satisfy Kuzovkin who has 'come into his estate' as both owner and father. For Olga it can only be sacrifice and loss.

Kuzovkin believes he has gained his identity, when in fact he has lost it. He has 'come into his estate' only in the most meaningless sense. Olga is left to escape alone to her room to weep over her own loss, while Tropachov congratulates Yeletski on his decency and generosity, no doubt harbouring thoughts of seducing his wife at the first opportunity. He and his parasitic double, Karpachov, have already become semi-permanent guests and he will no doubt batten on the family flesh with the same relish with which he tackled the meal in Act 1 – a parasite in a world of parasites. 'Nature . . . is the death of me', he announces at one point. Tropachov, is, indeed, symptomatic of dead nature in the debilitated world of the play as a whole.

The Bachelor

The Bachelor is unique among Turgenev's plays in having been written, published and performed all in the same year. It was also the first Turgenev play to be given a public performance. He composed it between January and March 1849 in Paris, from where he sent the manuscript to Shchepkin in Moscow. The play was permitted for the stage in October, although not before the censor had been to work with his blue pencil. A dialogue between Shpundik and Von Fonk about the difficult conditions prevailing in the countryside was excised, as was a speech by Moshkin in which he talked of the freedom and equality of women in marriage. All references to God were eliminated and certain names were changed – Von Fonk to Von Klaks and Belokopytova to Belonogova (literally Whitehoof to Whiteleg). The first performance was given for Shchepkin's benefit, on 14 October, at the Alexandrinski Theatre in St Petersburg with the beneficiary in the role of the minor official, Moshkin. It was a great success.

Turgenev's Plays 1848–1850

The basic situation in the three-act play concerns one Moshkin (*moshka* = midge), a fifty-year-old bachelor who has assumed the guardianship, since the death of her mother three years previously, of a nineteen-year-old girl, Masha. For more obscure reasons he has also assumed semi-parental responsibility for another orphan, Pyotr Vilitski, a twenty-three-year-old Petersburg minor official, and has contrived a match between them which is two weeks away from consummation at the opening of the play. During the course of the action Vilitski breaks off the engagement, largely under the influence of the above-mentioned Von Fonk, who appeals to his innate snobbery in suggesting that he could make a better match elsewhere. Dismayed by the outcome, Moshkin himself proposes marriage to his ward, a proposal which she half accepts, and Moshkin is left at the final curtain deliriously hopeful that something will come of this and that Masha will be happy.

Criticism and performance of *The Bachelor* appear bedevilled by some of the problems which also affect our understanding of *The Parasite*. In fact, the plays have a great deal in common, but not in the way in which these comparisons are traditionally made. The problem with the conventional way of seeing both *The Parasite* and *The Bachelor* seems to be the need to find positive elements in Turgenev's dramatic world with which to identify and sympathize. It has become traditional to see both Kuzovkin and Moshkin as representing a focus of moral opposition to the world around them. However, as in the case of Gogol, this is not the way in which Turgenev works. His method is essentially Gogolian in that the conflict is between negative elements in which the outcome is far from being so easily affirmative as criticism is inclined to suggest. The crucial element which has been missed in both *The Parasite* and *The Bachelor* is the way in which Turgenev has captured the spirit of Gogol's comedy of the grotesque and it is in this light that *The Bachelor*, in particular, needs to be viewed. To suggest that the play concerns another form of parasitism, that it is also about impotence and, again, about madness and that these themes are woven around the 'good' and 'kind-hearted' central character might raise a few eyebrows (possibly Turgenev's own). But this is the play he has demonstrably written and it is a much finer one than the play he is usually credited with being responsible for.

The first act introduces us to the milieu of Petersburg minor officialdom. The setting is Moshkin's apartment and Moshkin is at the centre of the action as he prepares a dinner party for the engaged couple and Vilitski's departmental colleague, Von Fonk. The dominant impression is of weirdness and eccentricity. The presence of both Masha and her aunt in what is a small bachelor apartment emphasizes the overcrowdedness. Moshkin's former sleeping accommodation appears to have been given over permanently to Masha, so that the reception room, where the first act is set, also functions as a bedroom for Moshkin – a corner of which is screened off. There is also a young servant, Stratilat, who, instead of occupying his traditional place in the hallway, appears to spend a good deal of his time lounging on his master's sofa. There is an all-pervading sense of curious incongruity. Under these conditions, cramped and chaotic, the master of the house manages his ménage in a fashion which might be appropriate in a country house, but which appears ludicrously out of place in the flat of a minor official in St Petersburg. The effect is of someone in thrall to the dictates of the values of his masters, whose ideals and codes of conduct he apes and aspires to emulate. The effect is of a *moshka* (midge) imitating a butterfly and the prospect is both absurd and grotesque.

The servant's speech at the opening of the play introduces us to the themes of education and enlightenment, which are referred to in various forms by several of the characters. Stratilat's level of 'enlightenment' consists in his struggling to pronounce that very word, syllable by syllable, in the book he is desperately trying to read, but which is frustrated by his constantly having to answer the bell. Moshkin's friend, Shpundik, is described by Turgenev as having 'pretensions to education'. Moshkin wishes to gain the approval of others by being associated with people of good upbringing and education. He wants Masha to be thought 'a queen' in society, as well as being anxious for Vilitski to work his way up the ladder of promotion in the civil service so that, eventually, Moshkin can claim a vicarious eminence through a form of kinship. Von Fonk represents that world of education and 'breeding' – the entirely false values which terrorize everyone else in the play and before which they pathetically abase themselves. This is represented through the forms of their dress, exaggerated to the point of caricature, their artificially mannered speech and in their sycophantic, intimidated humility in face of Von Fonk and everything he stands for.

The arrival of Shpundik, at the beginning of the play, also introduces the theme of 'Time'. In the world of the first act, everything is seen to move at a breathtaking, unnatural speed, with everybody consulting their watches and wondering what time it is from minute to minute. It all amounts to a portrait of Petersburg bureaucratic life, and its unnatural spirit is proportionately reflected in the artificial behaviour which such consciousness of time imposes on those whose movements are dictated by the tick of the clock. The manic impression is especially noticeable in the behaviour of Moshkin, whose characteristics are distinctly puppet-like. Against this is set the discussion of mortality between Shpundik and Moshkin, in which Turgenev is surely echoing that between Shallow and Silence in Shakespeare's *Henry IV, Part 2*.

In Moshkin's account of how he met Masha and her mother, rendered in comic-grotesque detail and style, complete with clown-like actions, we are introduced to another sense of 'Time'. Moshkin is always referring to himself as 'an old man'. His life is seemingly fixated on his relationship with the young couple and his desire to see them married. Equally, the actual duration of their acquaintance seems to be disproportionately short. Moshkin behaves as if at a crisis point in his own life. Well into middle-age, he appears to be seeking to live out his own unlived life vicariously, through the lives of the young people, and precipitately, because he feels he has not much time left. Time is making itself felt in Moshkin's own life with peculiar force. The childless bachelor, who has been a petty official all his life, suddenly seizes on a chance to live and, in the process, imposes his own necessities on the lives of two orphans who are unable to resist the pressures he exerts. What appears as altruism is, when looked at more closely, a form of parasitism which is entirely, if unconsciously, selfish.

Moshkin is also obsessed with his own inferiority and lack of distinction. This sense stems directly from a total acceptance, even worship, of a false society's evaluation of what constitutes distinction and superiority. Again, he seeks these qualities vicariously through the ambition he has for Vilitski's advancement. 'He will soon be titled', he tells Shpundik in a confidential whisper, 'he has a good and extensive acquaintance' and 'he works alongside the minister himself.' Vilitski's marriage to Masha can be seen as calculated, less to confer status on this girl of 'inferior' birth than to confer potency and social status on Moshkin by proxy through its association with his own surrogate parenthood and tutelage.

The entry of Von Fonk introduces us to the values of that wider external world which exerts such intense pressures and exercizes such power over the interior world of the play. Moshkin is moved to tears for reasons which he cannot explain by the visit of this supercilious and punctilious bureaucrat. The reason is not far to seek. It is as if a monarch had condescended to visit his humble abode. Moshkin is touched for his own sake, not for Masha's. In the pre-lunch conversation, he reveals himself as the perfect would-be bourgeois in his conduct of the deadeningly banal conversation and in his attempts to cover up any hiatus in the flow, while preserving an impression of surface calm. Underneath, a kind of inner panic reigns in the hearts of all as they seek to impress the imperturbable Von Fonk. When the latter actually tells his story, which concludes with the profound observation that 'there are people who look alike', Turgenev reveals him for the superficial fool he is.

The underlying madness comes to the surface when the decorum is threatened by the cook, Malanya, who comes to announce that dinner is ready. The stage directions indicate that Moshkin runs to bar her entrance 'in a frenzy; placing his knee in her stomach' like a mad major-domo. He then turns rapidly to his guests and with sycophantic nicety asks: 'Does anybody require anything else?' as if the breach of etiquette had been a figment of everyone's imagination.

The opening of Act 2 shows us the impoverished conditions in which Vilitski lives and which he clearly wishes to climb out of. Again the sense of grotesque parody is apparent in the incongruity of setting and behaviour. Vilitski orders his pipe to be brought as if he were seigneur of a chateau, while his throwing aside of the book with the words 'upbringing is a very important thing' serves to underline the hypocrisy of his reasons for rejecting Masha, ostensibly on the grounds of *her* lack of education, when his decision is in fact dictated by social snobbery. At the same time, what seems simply affectation can also be seen as a form of resistance to Moshkin's imposition of a match which is not of his own choosing. The values which Vilitski accepts are those of Von Fonk, who is shown to be providing him with an education in these values. The irony is, that in essence, they are indistinguishable from Moshkin's and, in many respects, echo him:

> I have already told you about my rule to avoid getting acquainted with people of the lower classes; from this rule, there naturally follows another, namely: try as hard as you can to become acquainted with people of the upper classes.

says Von Fonk. And this is the path which Vilitski chooses to follow, a logical extension of Moshkin's own wishes for him, with the exception that Masha will need to be replaced by someone who will make 'a better marriage'.

In the scene between Masha and Vilitski at the latter's apartment, in Act 2, Vilitski is more conscious of his concealed and eavesdropping guests in the adjoining room than he is of Masha's emotional plea. The scene has a Dickensian element of caricature which Masha's mispronunciation of the word 'examine' as 'ixamine', followed by Vilitski's wincing response, emphasizes. Turgenev, to a degree, invites us to share the laughter of those in the next room who can scarcely contain themselves. During the course of the subsequent interview between Vilitski and Moshkin, it emerges that the latter is less troubled by whether Vilitski loves her or not, than by whether he intends going through with the wedding. It is 'what people will think and say' which principally concerns him.

Moshkin's anger, in Act 3, is of a similar order. It is manifested less for Masha's sake than for his own. It is *his* protégé, as he sees it, who has been rejected by society. His decision to challenge Vilitski to a duel is deliberately rendered comic, as well as absurdly inappropriate, by Turgenev. It is interesting that Moshkin's response is already more like that of a husband than a father, but this only serves to redouble the irony. His challenge is only apt if the opponent is seen as a rival in love. In this case, the rival has *rejected* the loved one. The whole is a grotesque inversion of any recognizable norm. In this context, the most grotesque aspect of all is Moshkin's decision to propose to Masha.

This is the most critical scene in the play. Despite her rejection, it is clear that Masha still loves Vilitski and hopes that he will change his mind. At the same time, she recognizes that there is little hope. She clutches at his letter like a drowning person. Moshkin already knows the contents but, in his present state of feeling, wants the contents to kill off the vestigial love. When she reads the confirmation of rejection, Masha stifles in that same moment the possibility of ever loving again. There is nothing left in life to hope for. Yet who is it who is responsible for evoking this love and inspiring this hope? Who is to blame? It is not Vilitski, but the man who stands before her offering himself as a substitute marriage partner.

Moshkin describes himself as 'losing his mind' and as 'a madman' and, indeed, in an important sense he is. It is plain that Masha has been merely instrumental in furthering his wider claims for recognition and significance. Now that this possibility no longer exists, the wider social ambition shrinks to the compass of the narrow arena of the apartment. In fact, fantasy takes over as a substitute for an unattainable 'reality':

> All I want to do is to prove to the world, that to marry you is the height of happiness . . . That's what I want to prove to the world – that is, to Pyotr Ilyich . . . I offer you, then, peace, quiet, respect, shelter. . . . Here, you will be a mistress, a madam, a lady. . . .

and he adds, in pathetic acknowledgement of his own impotence which puts a seal on the barren prospects before her:

> . . . and I . . . the screens, you understand, the screens, and nothing further. . . .

Masha does not agree to marry him but agrees to stay for the time being:

> You will not deceive me: you will not betray me. I can depend on you.

And she gives him cause for hope.

Once again, we see the woman as victim. For someone whose own hope, not to say her whole life, has been shattered to smithereens, faced with the person who is the Svengali-like cause of her suffering, Masha's offer to him of hope in return is fraught with irony. Moshkin's condition towards the end of the play is surely not the one traditionally rendered in performance. His manifestation of joy is close to dementia. Pryazhkina clearly thinks he has had a stroke:

Why, his face is all twisted, and his lips too. He has had a stroke.

He stands as someone condemned to hope and to the belief that his life may now begin to take on meaning. But he himself recognizes that '. . . it's a dream, an illusion'. His final cry: 'She will be happy! She will be happy! is less a cry of joyful determination than an attempt to drown the recognition of hopelessness and despair in the face of the ruin which is his own life, and the ruin he has brought on the lives of others.

Lunch with the Marshal of the Nobility

It is probably true to say that there is little evidence in his prose work that Turgenev was, potentially, a comic writer of considerable stature. There is certainly nothing in his novels or short stories which has the comic liveliness of his play *Lunch with the Marshal of the Nobility*, one of the funniest Russian comedies of the nineteenth century. Like *Moneyless*, it shows evidence of a strong debt to the techniques of vaudeville as well as to the plays and short stories of Gogol. In the humour of the quarrel over estate boundaries, the play anticipates the Chekhov of *The Proposal*, but without ever becoming quite as farcical.

The action of the one-act play takes place on the estate

of Marshal of the Nobility, Balagalayev, whom the disputants, Bespandin and his widowed sister Kaurova, have turned to in the hope of a rapid resolution (rather than a protracted legal wrangle) of a problem over estate division. The marshalship, an honorary post, was subject to election on a short-term basis by the landowners of a specific region. Balagalayev's rival for the marshalship is one Pekhterev, who also becomes involved in the resolution of this particular dispute and introduces a subsidiary theme of the rivalry between the two marshals, incumbent and presumptive. A third theme is introduced in the person of Alupkin, newly arrived in the district from Tambov, who is in dispute with the district inspector, Naglanovich, as to whether it is one of his (Alupkin's) peasants who is responsible for stealing a goat. Beneath the surface of this farcical plot the currents of the play run deep.

It was originally written for Nekrasov's *The Contemporary* but was forbidden publication by the censor. Surprisingly, the play was passed for stage performance and the first production was given at the Alexandrinski Theatre in December 1849. The sub-title of the first performed version was 'An Amicable Division', but, despite its success, it was not permitted publication until 1856, by which time Turgenev had revised it and weakened it considerably (this is the version which has come down to us). The first version is said to have been more actable than the final, published version. The original script contained very precise directions from the author as to intonations and group dispositioning on stage – for example at the moments when the map of the estate is consulted. Reference to a 'dumb-scene' (presumably influenced by *The Government Inspector*) is omitted from the published version, as is a story which Mirvoshkin

Turgenev's Plays 1848–1850

(Mirvolin in the published edition) tells about his wife, and a scene where some of the characters imitate the gobbling of turkeys. Bespandin was depicted in far more grotesque fashion in the original, where he is described as stuffing his mouth with both hands while feeding, and spitting, whistling and so forth.

The background to the play involves last-ditch attempts by the authorities to prop up a collapsing feudal order by clarifying boundary divisions between estates. Where owners died intestate and there were several legal claimants to the estate, the resulting litigation as to the precise extent of what each inherited became a legal nightmare. Turgenev focuses the dispute on close relatives in order to reinforce a connection between a process of division and separation in the social sphere and the way in which this is reflected in internecine strife within families. The point which forms the centre of the action, and which is referred to at the end of the play, is not that an amicable 'settlement' has been reached (as M. S. Mandell's translation has it) but, ironically, an amicable 'division' or 'partition'. The agreement is to divide and separate, not to unite. The official appointed by the government to assist in the determination of these disputes appears as a *deus ex machina* at the end of the play but, typically and comically, is unable to resolve the difficulty.

The major theme of the play is division, in society and in the family. Within this sense of division there is also the theme of separation between male and female, as well as that of inheritance. Colouring each strand and interwoven with them is a refrain repeated from *The Parasite* and *The Bachelor* – that of madness. The amiable farce is concerned with disintegration and breakdown in both the social and personal spheres. We are, once again, in territory already made familiar by Gogol.

The incipient insanity in the play is an aspect of the obsessiveness of the characters. Balagalayev is obsessed with his status and privately concerned with the personal advantage to be gained from the settlement which he is ostensibly superintending as impartial arbiter. His personality is inherently fragile and the chorus of conflicting demands produces an inner fragmentation in his being. He reaches the point of breakdown near the end:

> I beg of you, my head's swimming . . . Division, a goat, obstinate woman, Tambov landowner, unexpected district inspector, a duel tomorrow, my conscience isn't clear, the estate, cut-price woods, lunch, noise, confusion . . . no, it's too much.

Alupkin is obsessed by four things – the goat which his peasant is supposed to have stolen, his dislike of women revealed through his attitude to Kaurova, his status as 'an old soldier', and the fact that he has managed to father a daughter. Pekhterev is obsessed with the marshalship. His apparent favouritism towards Kaurova has nothing to do with the merits of her case, but is a stance adopted simply in order to upset his rival, Balagalayev. He is also upset because the session has begun without him.

Bespandin is obsessed with winning the quarrel over the division of the estates. His apparent willingness to compromise is because he knows the cards are stacked against his sister as all the arbitrators present are male. He himself is unmarried. The only person who is not obsessed is the one who stands accused of incurable obstinacy, Kaurova. She is the only one who can conceivably be described as 'acting' the part she is playing – of 'stubborn female', 'helpless widow', 'put-upon litigant and *faux-naif* disputant'. The men are as if enclosed in the roles they play and unable to see beyond themselves to the insane ludicrousness of the situation. Kaurova not only understands but wilfully stretches the logic of the general insanity beyond the point where any normal person would go, just for the pleasure of watching the men pass beyond this point. She is far from being stubborn and is, in fact, so flexible that the men are incapable of noticing. There is a key point in the play, half-way through, immediately before the entry of Pekhterev. Up until this point, Bespandin's apparent flexibility has been countered at every turn by the sister's apparent stubbornness. They have reached a point of impasse. At this juncture Kaurova declares: 'I'll agree to anything. Let me have the papers. I'll sign anything you want me to!' – a remark which is completely ignored by all present.

Nearly everybody at some stage is described as 'mad' – Bespandin, his sister, Alupkin, even the aunt who left the will. Bespandin challenges Alupkin to a duel to defend the honour of his family, while simultaneously declaring that he doesn't give 'that much' for his sister. Pekhterev's suggestion that he make sacrifices because his sister is a woman, he answers with: 'That's only in theory'. Alupkin declares that nothing would surprise him any more – even if someone were to announce, 'I have eaten my own father!' Finally the desperate Balagalayev forgives the cause of his despair, Kaurova, *because* she is a woman. In the atmosphere of exaggeration, charge and countercharge, Kaurova chimes in with an assertion that her brother is a murderer who is prepared to cut her throat and has already tried to poison her several times. As the chorus mounts, the district inspector enters and is immediately assumed by the self-preoccupied Alupkin to be there on account of the goat. This individualistic interpretation signals the point of breakdown for Balagalayev, who lists the fragments of a fragmenting world in the speech already quoted.

A final irony concerns that which remains in dispute, namely the possession of 'waste land', which connects with Alupkin's inheritance of his wife's estate, described as 'absolute rubbish . . . just sand'. The play's last line: 'That's what I call an amicable division! . . .' underwrites the incongruity and absurdity of the action.

A Provincial Lady

A Provincial Lady was written in 1850 and published in *Notes of The Fatherland* in 1851, an event which had been preceded by public readings of the work given by Turgenev himself, with great success, at various private houses in St Petersburg and Moscow. Described as 'a comedy in one act', *A Provincial Lady* looks at first glance, very much like a trivial French-inspired vaudeville.

The plot is certainly typical. Darya Ivanovna, the twenty-eight-year-old wife of Stupendyev, a very conventional district government clerk twenty years her senior, has lived the eight or so years of her married life in a boring provincial town with only a cook, a houseboy and a nineteen-year-old male distant cousin for company, for the last-mentioned of whom she has assumed the role of benefactress. She, in her turn, was reared as a humble ward in the home of *her* benefactress, a local countess, since deceased, and retains memories of other ways of life as well as of her youthful ambitions. These are revived by a return visit to his country estate of the countess's son, Count Lyubin, now an ageing dandy of forty-nine who, some ten years previously, had flirted in a casual fashion with the young ward whilst on leave from the military. His affairs in St Petersburg appear to have taken a turn for the worse and he needs to consult the local district government officer (Darya's husband) about matters concerning his late mother's estate. The young wife exploits this opportunity to remind the count of their erstwhile connection and to exploit her now mature powers of sexual charm to gain for both herself and her husband, as well as her ward, positions in the more glamorous world of St Petersburg. This she manages to do, although her husband's jealousy (he is not informed of his wife's plot) nearly undoes the whole scheme as well as leading to the count's enlightenment as to the young wife's subterfuge. Despite this, the play concludes on a happy note as the group exits for dinner and the count looks forward to their next meeting – in the capital.

The play is far from being as superficial as the plot outline may make it sound. In it, Turgenev reveals himself to be not only a precursor of a minor revolution in dramatic form, but also a forerunner of the master of domestic drama in the nineteenth century, Henrik Ibsen. Just as, through the surface texture of the domestic drama, Ibsen reaches beyond a surface realism towards something altogether more abstract, so Turgenev manages something very similar in *A Provincial Lady*, although the emotional colouring of the drama is much lighter than the darkness which can be detected in the Norwegian dramatist. Another important connection with later drama, and in particular with the Symbolists, lies in Turgenev's recognition of the puppet-show elements which underlie the ostensibly realistic surface of human actions.

There are strong parallels between the domestic worlds of *A Provincial Lady* and *A Doll's House*, *Hedda Gabler* and even *Rosmersholm*. The connecting link is through the remarkable character of Darya Ivanovna. Through her, the play becomes a drama of the phenomenal and thwarted power of woman, but without the serious consequences which this is shown to have in Ibsen's plays. There is a persistent sense, in Ibsen, that the typical nineteenth-century woman sitting at her knitting, or at the embroidery frame, is simultaneously weaving the pattern of fate which will engulf the protagonists at the conclusion. In this respect, Darya Ivanovna possesses some of the power of Rebecca West in *Rosmersholm* and, at the outset, is shown sitting at her embroidery from where she appears to conduct the sequence of events which follows. She assumes the role of the man, just as Hedda and Nora Helmer do, and her relationship with her husband has much in common with that between the women and the conventional, weak men in Ibsen's plays. Everyone who comes within her reach comes under her extraordinary spell and moves in the way she wants them to, prompted by a hand gesture or a nod; or else they come under the magnetic influence of her powerful sexual attraction.

Although the play is a comedy and the resolution appears trivial and rather unsatisfactory, Turgenev manages to convey a sense, if not of tragedy, then of waste of human energy and paucity of ambition. It is stressed that the desire to leave this provincial backwater and move to St Petersburg is merely trivial. It is implied, that in this kind of society, the energy of a Darya Ivanovna either lies dormant or can only be purposeless and without direction, determined, to a large extent, by the ideological ambience of aristocratic taste which nurtures it and in which she has been reared. These values are both subconsciously recognized as worthless and, as if prompted by environmental determinism, simultaneously striven for. The resolution of the problem is not, as in Ibsen, on the level of tragedy but on a level of absurdity. It has the effect of reducing the world, as experienced by the central character, to the proportions of a puppet show in a fairground, a kind of *bouffonade*.

With brilliant originality, Turgenev manages to convert the realistic milieu into a kind of miniature 'theatre of the mind', which is a grotesque reflection of the ostensible normality of everyday appearances. Just as, in *Hedda Gabler*, the inner room with its curtains across it, which separate it from the rest of the setting and in which Hedda commits suicide, represents the theatre of *her* mind, similarly, in *A Provincial Lady* everything appears filtered through the consciousness of the central protagonist. In the process, what emerges is a fairly light-hearted puppet show, in which Darya Ivanovna is revealed as the puppet master, while being herself subject to certain manipulative constraints.

Turgenev manages to suggest the reduction in physical scale, reminiscent of a fairground booth, through details of the stage setting, which suggest not only constriction but also diminution. It is the world of the doll's house as seen from the adult height of Darya Ivanovna, but where the rest of the characters are of a size proportionate to the environment. The garden, *sad*, is given in the opening stage directions as a *sadik* (tiny little garden), the table *stol* is described as a *stolik* (tiny little table), the piano is 'small', the screen 'low' and one can imagine the rest of the setting in equivalent terms. The puppet-show element is then carried over into the characterization. The houseboy (named Apollo) is kitted out in light-blue livery which does not fit him. He manifests one permanent emotion, fear, and keeps poking his head round doors, rapidly exiting into adjoining rooms or is seen emerging from them in flight. The count is described in terms of a doll. Not only is his every move dictated by Darya Ivanovna, but his hair is dyed and his face is powdered and rouged, like the painted image of a clown. When he gets down on his knees, it is as if his 'wooden' legs lack the muscle power to get him to his feet again. He eventually leaps up, apparently under his own volition, but the impression is of someone being jerked to his feet on strings. It is a critical moment. Darya Ivanovna's suppressed laughter threatens to make the grotesquerie of the characters permanent. In restoring the count to his feet (seemingly by an act of will on *her* part, not on his) and in laughing openly, demonstratively, Darya Ivanovna restores to some kind of normality the marionette world whose scenario she has written. The puppet-like nature of the husband has characteristics in common with the count. He wears a wig which, when removed, one imagines reveals a perfectly bald head, like that of a wooden doll. At one point he provides us with a glimpse of his marionette-like status when complaining about the cut of his coat: 'I feel as though I were being dragged up on a string'.

Movement in the play, when it is not precipitate, has all the formal characteristics of marionettes. People seem to be constantly propelled to their feet, jerkily bowing, materializing in doorways, parading up and down on seemingly involuntary impulse. The power of the theatre holds sway over all and the only person who is aware of this power and is consciously exploiting it is Darya Ivanovna. She is congratulated by the count, following the restoration of 'normality', on how well she has 'played her comedy'. People are provided with their roles and told when to make their entrances. At one point, Stupendyev enters before his cue. Darya Ivanovna is like a female Gulliver in Lilliput, pinned to the ground by constraining threads, but maintaining a hold on strings attached to each Lilliputian figure in the drama she has staged and directed.

Turgenev's Plays 1848–1850

There is the major problem of Darya Ivanovna's involvement in the world she ridicules. With part of herself she *does* seek to advance her husband's position in the social world of St Petersburg and 'save' him, as Nora does Torvald. In flirting with the count she is also, in a rather trivial way, seeking to confirm a sense of her own attractiveness at twenty-eight (which she sees as more than half-way to the grave). There is also a feeling that, in fairly petty fashion, she is avenging an earlier humiliation when the count appears to have trifled with her affections, evidence of which she retains in the form of a letter he once wrote to her. Her attempt to exercise power over him is experienced as a form of victory, whereas we have learned from a play such as *Where It's Thin, There It Breaks* that to win can be, in fact, to lose and that there may be more to be gained from losing than from winning. She becomes part of this reduced world, significantly, when we see her *on her own* and when the stage in the theatre of her mind is occupied by the image of herself, soliloquizing while getting ready for 'battle', or posing before the mirror and dreaming of exchanging her simple dress for something in velvet, more in keeping with St Petersburg. This, of course, is also Hedda Gabler's problem – one of trivially snobbish ambition, and an aspect of the many contradictory sides to her nature which can only find resolution in suicide. There is a suggestion in *A Provincial Lady* that the contemplated move to St Petersburg may be a form of suicide or, at least, will certainly end in disillusionment.

The actor at the Moscow Art Theatre who played the part of Darya's ward, Misha, in the 1912 production, A. D. Diki, suggests, in his published account of work on the play, that Stanislavski instinctively felt this sense of *bouffonade* and certainly managed to capture it in his portrayal of Lyubin. It is precisely this element of caricature which was criticized at the time by commentators who had come to expect their Turgenev to be served up in conventionally realistic fashion. It is interesting to note that the designer was M. V. Dobuzhinski who had designed Potyomkin's *Petrushka* for Meyerhold in St Petersburg, in 1908, in the style of a quasi-grotesque puppet show. In *My Life In Art*, Stanislavski suggests that there was a dispute between himself and Dobuzhinski over the kind of image Lyubin was to present, especially in the manner in which his face was to be made up. The implication is that the approach of the actors at this stage was in terms of their preparatory work on *A Month in the Country* (that is, within the psychologically realistic framework of Stanislavski's development of the 'system') and that Dobuzhinski's suggestion as to the physical make-up and appearance of the count was altogether more schematic and simplified, based, Stanislavski suggested, on unfamiliarity with the text and on insufficient knowledge of the theatre's working methods. [4] However, that which finally emerged in performance appears to have been something closer to Dobuzhinski's schematicism than a clear product of the 'system'.

It was in a mood of doubt and despair that Stanislavski suggested that the cast put on a special performance for the theatre's other artistic director V. Nemirovich-Danchenko and, as a consequence of this, he was forced to re-think his whole approach to the play, and to move away from the previous style towards something altogether more original. 'Why did Turgenev call the play *A Provincial Lady* and not "Provincial Life" or "A Provincial Story"? was the question posed by Nemirovich-Danchenko, and it was as a result of this that a shift in emphasis was brought about in the overall conception, more in keeping with the ironical intentions of Turgenev's writing. The theme then became the *contrast* between the provincial surrounding and the ultra-sophistication of the provincial lady herself. From playing Lyubin as an aristocrat, Stanislavski began to convert him into an image of 'provincialism' masquerading as aristocracy. Everything was now framed in contrast to Darya Ivanovna with the result that, although she was not the main focus of the production, the theme of provincialism which the director had wanted to stress all along was thrown into much sharper focus. Even the notion of St Petersburg itself, symbol of nineteenth-century Russia, was drawn into the theme of 'provincialism as a way of life, as a mode of being' with its banality, its lack of vision and its 'profound hostility to any ray of talent'.[5] This was emphasized by the atmosphere of total boredom at the opening of the play and by stressing the clumsy gaucheness of the servants. Dobuzhinski's setting helped to convey the sense of a typically Russian provincial milieu, in which the dominant colour was a rather tasteless yellow with a view through the window of the town beyond, with its naïve-looking church.

Stanislavski's approach to the role of Lyubin gradually developed away from the realistic portrayal of a decayed aristocrat towards the style of the *bouffonade*. Critics who noticed this took him to task for it while others closer to the Art Theatre, such as N. E. Efros, detected these elements in the play itself, quite rightly, and described Stanislavski's creation as a genuine work of art:

> Stanislavski brought out in the character everything which was archetypically comic, everything which is close, namely, to the 'buffo'. . . . The caricature grew to the level of an artistic creation.[6]

8
'A Month in the Country'

Turgenev's international reputation as a dramatist rests, almost entirely, on his five-act comedy *A Month in the Country*, the one play to be both widely translated and performed. In many ways, it is ironic that this, his most popular play, should have been considered by many nineteenth-century writers and critics to be inferior to his other dramatic work and that Turgenev himself considered it to be more of a novel in play form than a drama. It is, perhaps, significant that the play's reputation derives less from critical evaluations of its intrinsic merits than from the history of memorable productions (often adaptations or reduced versions of the play), the most famous of which was the Moscow Art Theatre production in 1909, directed by Stanislavski. It was, more or less, as a consequence of this production that Turgenev was rediscovered for the twentieth century as a dramatist and came to be regarded as an important forerunner, as far as dramatic method was concerned, of Chekhov. However, Turgenev's plays generally have little in common with

'A Month in the Country'

those of Chekhov. Apart from superficial links between the 'contrapuntalism' exploited by Chekhov in a play such as *Three Sisters* and comparable moments in *A Month in the Country*, the main connections between the two dramatists are thematic rather than technical, especially in the contrast which both emphasize between the larger world of Nature and the circumscribed world of human beings. This is a major theme of Turgenev's fiction, prefigured to some extent in his last major drama.

Written in 1850, its first title was *The Student*. Submitted to *The Contemporary*, it ran into censorship problems which were to prevent performance on the stage for the next twenty-two years. The censor's main attack appears to have been on moral rather than political grounds. Objection was taken to the fact that Natalya Petrovna, a married woman, should form emotional attachments with two men in addition to her husband. It was put to Turgenev that he would do better to make her a widow. The censor was also unhappy about the student Belyayev's championing of the work of Belinski. This was more obvious in the original version, before the reference was revised to the present suggestion of his liking for critical articles written by a 'warm-blooded person'. All references to the social conditions of the time were eliminated, including a whole section, in Act 4, where Shpigelski the doctor went into details of his impoverished childhood.

The second draft of the play was re-christened *Two Women* but it too was prohibited. A third version was prepared in December 1854, under its present title *A Month in the Country* and, after some further excisions demanded by the censor, was finally granted permission for publication, but not performance, in 1855. The play was included in the 1869 edition of his 'Scenes and

Comedies' where, in a foreword, Turgenev noted that *A Month in the Country* now appeared for the first time in its original form. This was not entirely accurate. References to Shpigelski having had to go 'barefoot about the streets' as a child, and to his mother, because of the family's poverty, having been forced to wear an old army greatcoat while the children awaited her arrival home with the 'craving hunger of young wolves' – all this, together with lines and phrases considered derogatory to the landed classes, were excluded from the final version by Turgenev himself as an act of self-censorship.

The first stage production of the play was at the Maly Theatre, Moscow, on 13 January 1872. Turgenev was in Paris at the time where he received cuttings of the newspaper reviews sent him by his brother, Nikolai. He was not surprised by the almost universally bad reception the play was given:

> . . . my comedy . . . deserved to be a fiasco. It is for that reason that . . . I have given up writing for the stage; it is not for me.[1]

Seven years later, in 1879, the play was to have its first great success on the stage. The event has entered the annals of Russian theatre history and was especially memorable for the superb performance of Marya Savina in the comparatively small part of Vera.

Abortive novel or play, *A Month in the Country* contains magnificent material for actors, as do all Turgenev's dramas – a fact which makes their neglect even more incomprehensible. Apart from its Russian performances, *A Month in the Country* has been staged with great success all over the world and especially in Britain and America where actors and audiences familiar with English inter-

'A Month in the Country'

pretations of Chekhov have found that the play's country house setting and characters can be gracefully accommodated on the professional stage.

The widespread availability of Emlyn Williams's 'version' of *A Month in the Country*, in two acts, prepared for his own production of the play at the St James's Theatre, London, in 1943, as opposed to Constance Garnett's translation of the full-length five-act original, is sufficient evidence of how inadequate a dramatist Turgenev is considered to be. This is the only generally available English translation of the play and it has been reprinted six times. It is only necessary to imagine a comparable situation existing in respect of a play such as Chekhov's *Three Sisters* to appreciate that, for English-speaking audiences, Turgenev is known second-hand at best and that there exists an assumption that he is a failed dramatist who needs to be rendered more 'theatrical'. The question remains – how good or bad a play is the original *A Month in the Country*?

The generally held opinion among English-speaking critics is re-stated by Turgenev's most recent biographer, Leonard Schapiro, when he argues that:

> It is beyond question Turgenev's only play with a claim to dramatic distinction. The charge of bookishness can justly be levelled at the earlier plays, but *A Month in the Country* is of absorbing psychological subtlety, and rivets the attention, even if its action is limited.[2]

Richard Freeborn, in his distinguished study of Turgenev the novelist, repeats the suggestion that the play was 'to form the basis of Chekhov's dramaturgy', whilst pointing to its influence on Turgenev's own later novel writing:

But it is the nuances of dialogue, the incongruities of personal relationship and the characteristic, atmospheric flavour, which distinguish the work. Turgenev's experience from writing this five-act comedy was to prove invaluable to him in matters of construction and dialogue when he came to write his novels.[3]

Most staged versions of the play have taken for granted that it is too long and have either made substantial cuts in the text or, as in the recent Soviet production by Anatoli Efros, have eliminated the four complicated scene changes between each act by presenting the play 'symbolically', in this instance as a Russian version of *La Ronde*, with almost the entire action taking place on a wrought-iron carousel, set in motion by the bored participants in the love-game whenever their jaded emotions sense the need for stimulation. It is the only play of Turgenev's in which his characters tend to soliloquize at considerable length. Directors have either cut these lengthy self-revelatory monologues or reduced them considerably, although Michael Redgrave, who knows the play well from the point of view of both actor and director, considers the soliloquies to be 'of an extraordinarily fine, silken subtlety'.[4]

A Month in the Country reflects the changes which overtook Turgenev's creative writing in the early 1850s when, with his plays misunderstood, misinterpreted and censored, he abandoned the public world of the stage for the private and more introspective world of the novel. As such, *A Month in the Country* may be described as a *novel manqué*, and stands as an attempt to render the psychological intricacies of the nineteenth-century realistic novel in a form for which it is not ideally suited. The tradition which has kept the play alive, dramatically, is one which

'A Month in the Country'

has long been preserved in the theatre, namely, that the purpose of theatre-going is to see great acting. As such, *A Month in the Country* has provided plenty of opportunities for the actor in a manner which is essentially similar to those which have been provided by dramatic adaptations of prose works such as *Rudin, On The Eve, Fathers and Sons* and *A Nest of Gentlefolk*, which have long been popular on the Russian stage.

A Month in the Country differs mainly from Turgenev's earlier drama in being concerned with themes which are explored in the world of the novels. Another difference might also be categorized as a variation in degree between optimism and pessimism, as the lighter, socially-contingent world of the plays moves into the darker, more pessimistically absolutist world of the novels. In this sense, *A Month in the Country* may be categorized as a transitional work, with the year 1850 marking a watershed in Turgenev's creative life and in his philosophical outlook. The themes which begin to carry the main burden of despair relate to the inevitable contrast between the apparently harmonious world of Nature and the discordant world of human beings governed by increasingly determinist criteria (Turgenev's friendship with the naturalist writer, Flaubert, is instructive), and to love seen as a source of poisonous infection, torment and destruction.

A Month in the Country explores some of the same territory as *Uncle Vanya*. The sense of naturalistic determinism which hovers in the background of Chekhov's play also haunts the margins of Turgenev's world. The disturbance of the quiet backwater caused by the arrival of the elderly professor and his young wife in Vanya's household has similarities with the effect produced by the arrival in the Islayevs' rural idyll of the young tutor, Belyayev. It is almost as if, as in *Uncle Vanya* (and, incidentally, in some of Strindberg's plays), the characters are treated as chemical constituents which, mixed in a particular crucible, will, according to some predetermined principle, produce such-and-such a chemical reaction. From this perspective, the introduction of Belyayev resembles a bacillus which, injected into the foreign body of this environment, will give rise to the 'infection' or 'disease' of love. The 'month' in the country, under these conditions, becomes less a time of escapist lyricism, than a period of incubation. It is constantly to the naturalistic undertow of this world that Turgenev refers with his 'dramatic' consciousness, while his 'novelist' self is concerned with the psychologically real, elaborately rich and sophisticated surface of another area of life.

It is a world of sexual awakening as well as one of repression. It is also an arena of sexual battle. The world of nature does not exactly revenge itself on the characters but, as in the novels, is simply indifferent or throws their behaviour into ironic contrast. Nothing could be more ironic than the choice of Belyayev as, in some sense, epitomizing 'naturalness' and vitality, the 'fresh air' which wafts through the drama or 'the glass of cold water on a hot day' which Natalya Petrovna longs for. He is, in fact, more like someone suffering himself from an acute sense of repression, underlined by his reverting in this more 'natural' context to childhood pastimes, or indulging in symbolic acts of tree-climbing, shaking down innocent wild life in order to set the dogs on it, mounting cattle, or, armed with a rifle, setting out to destroy wild birds. As Michael Redgrave noted in Anmer Hall's production at the Festival Theatre, Cambridge, when Katya offered Belyayev the raspberries in Act 2: '. . . they became the apple in the garden of Eden'.[5] He could also have noted that Belyayev is the serpent which has entered this

'A Month in the Country'

demi-paradise and it can be no accident that one of the child-like activities which Turgenev has him indulge in is flying a kite – in Russian *zapuskat' zmeya* which literally means 'to release a serpent'. Human repression, constraint, embarrassment and shame are stressed throughout. Accompanying the desire to relate is the terror of relationship and the inability, finally, for human beings to find harmonious sexual and spiritual contact with each other. Turgenev has Islayev, Natalya's husband, symbolically constructing a dam in the background, as if to stem the tide of human feelings and to repress the natural forces welling up within them.

It is a traditional feature of Russian criticism to regard Belyayev as a positive force in the play, to see him as a representative of the disenfranchized *raznochintsy* (nineteenth-century intellectuals of non-aristocratic origin), an intellectual with a strong resemblance to Belinski. He is also frequently equated with Bazarov, the scientific, positivist hero of *Fathers and Sons*. There is some truth in this latter identification, in that Belyayev shares some of Bazarov's contempt for poetry and appears unaware of the irrational power of love which, like an infection, takes possession of both of them against their will. However, compared with the tragic nature of Bazarov's fate, Belyayev's presents an almost comic contrast. The revelation of Natalya's love for him produces not only the chemical change in his psychological make-up, but also the comic change in his physical appearance when he appears the following morning in his best jacket with a flower in the button-hole. Belyayev's inexperience and naïveté are contrasted with the more mature suffering of his 'rival', Rakitin, whose permanently elegant exterior masks the inner sickness of his ineffectual love. His description of the humiliating nature of his torment and the indignity of his role is couched, tellingly, in terms of 'calamity', 'torture', 'enslavement', 'poison' and 'slavery'.

A persistent feature of the play, as of the later novels, is Turgenev's new fatalistic sense that life can only be lived as a version of farce or comedy and that, even at its most intensely serious moments, something will occur to undermine its dignity or to display human suffering as both grotesque and comic. Rakitin speaks of 'keeping up a farce before each other', in conversation with Belyayev. Islayev's totally detached attitude towards his own feelings is ironically compared with Othello's jealousy, and Natalya Petrovna speaks of 'the farce' which she has been acting, which revolts her. There is an aspect of the grotesque of the Commedia dell'Arte about Shpigelski, the *dottore*, as he engineers a marriage between the young, beautiful Vera and the *pantalone* Bolshintsov, ageing and stupid, in return for a gift of horses. Shpigelski's engagement to Lizaveta Bogdanovna, the veiled announcement of which concludes the play, not only relates their 'love' to that of the protagonists but, through the relationship, undercuts and subverts the latter's ostensible dignity, like the presence of the doctor at Insarov's deathbed in *On The Eve*. Shpigelski's cynicism is stressed throughout and the rationalization of his unscrupulousness is relayed through his recognition of a naturalist world underlying all appearances and which he describes in a typically grotesque and theatrical fashion, like a performance in a clown-show, as he enacts his vision of the people of the estate:

(*capering about*) The grey wolves ate that little goat up,
   The grey wolves ate that little goat up,
      They ate him up, they ate him up,
         Yes, I say, they ate him up.

The physiological reality underlying the hothouse en-

'A Month in the Country'

vironment of these cultivated and vulnerable people is shown to erupt through the controlled surface in the form of nervous outbreaks, quarrels, hysteria, emotional outbursts. A sense of the fullness of aristocratic individualism becomes reduced to the underlying pattern of their nervous systems. This was very well conveyed in Toby Robertson's 1974 Chichester Festival Theatre production, where the vividly coloured zig-zag pattern on the upholstery seemed suggestive of a chart recording the nervous responses of the characters to stimuli, as if electrodes were attached to each.

Metaphors in the play relate to oppositions between sickness and health, storm and calm, swimming and drowning, arriving and departing, enlightenment and disillusion, responsibility and irresponsibility, the high and the low, the romantic and the real, youth and age. The problems arise from the attempt to contain these oppositions within a unified dramatic form (where the romantic is required to coexist with the realistic) and concern modes of perception as well as the question of Turgenev's relationship to the social group with which the play is concerned. This problem is encountered in more intense form by later naturalistic dramatists, such as Ibsen and Strindberg. The point can be illustrated by contrasting what, at first sight, seem very dissimilar plays, *A Month in the Country* and *Hedda Gabler*. In the latter play, the coexistence of the realistic and the grotesque, the romantic and the naturalistic are consciously integrated into the play's structure as a central aspect of the chief protagonist's vision – so that a character like Lovborg, for example, is dramatized in conscious fashion by Ibsen as, simultaneously, 'romantic hero' and 'feckless reprobate', as 'independent individual' and 'dependent puppet'. It needs to be demonstrated that the heroine's vicarious longing for life and the world of noble action finds an *ironic* focus in Lovborg. The same kind of irony is latent in the depiction of Belyayev in *A Month in the Country*, but is not so consciously worked.

The same may be said of Turgenev's depiction of Natalya's relations with her husband, which share some of the same unsatisfactory elements as those of Hedda and Tesman. Turgenev's ironic detachment from the milieu he depicts is not as distant or as condemnatory as Ibsen's, but that is the direction in which the drama is moving. It is noticeable that Chekhov appears to have learned his lessons from Ibsen, rather than from Turgenev when, in *The Cherry Orchard*, he dramatizes the superannuated social world of *A Month in the Country* as farce rather than as a psychologically convincing, ideologically sustaining version of aristocratic reality.[6] The problems which *A Month in the Country* presents have usually been resolved, in production, by reconciling its inner contradictions on the level of a higher order of reality, with an emphasis on 'sensibility', rather than natural impulse, on romance rather than realism. As far as the twentieth century is concerned, the pattern appears to have been established by the approach to characterization which governed the conception of the Moscow Art Theatre production in 1909.

The decision to stage the play was reached at a time when Stanislavski was first beginning to develop the theories which gave rise to the famous 'system'; at a point where his focus was shifting from an emphasis on external, naturalistic detail in performance towards a concentration on the inner, psychological authenticity of emotional feeling, allied to such concepts as the 'through line of action' and the 'ruling idea' of a play, as well as the 'pieces

'A Month in the Country'

and problems' of particular sections. As he explained later in *My Life In Art*:

> What directed us towards Turgenev, who had long been denied as a dramatist? We needed a play of complex psychology for laboratory work.

The emphasis was clearly to be on the 'spiritual' side of the play, accepting the psychological reality of the characters very much in the manner of a typical nineteenth-century novel. What needed to be demonstrated, according to Stanislavski, was:

> . . . immobility and the absence of gesture . . . so as to display the inner essence and the word-picture of the spiritual lacework of Turgenev.

To achieve this, he demanded a style of virtuoso acting from his cast to facilitate the spectators,

> . . . entering into the souls of the actors through the eyes . . . [and] receiving through the voice and its intonations the inner essence of the feelings and thoughts of the characters in the play.

The quasi-mystical aspect of this approach appears borne out by his additional remarks to the effect that:

> One needed some sort of unseen emanation of creative will, emotion, longing; one needed eyes, mimetics, hardly palpable intonations of the voice, psychological pauses.[7]

This highly experimental approach to the play perhaps

needs to be related, in salutary fashion, to similar kinds of experimentation which other directors were conducting at the time into Symbolist forms of theatre, and into the theatre of masks. Here, however, they were adopting approaches which tended to emphasize the physical, external aspects of dramatic characterization, scorning individual psychology in favour of the grotesquerie of Commedia dell'Arte or more stylized forms of representation.

Stanislavski wanted a production which was very much in the style of the epoch in which the play is set – the beginning of the 1840s – and, to this end, invited M. V. Dobuzhinski of the 'World of Art' group to do the designs. The result was something which, in terms of surface aestheticism and sheer visual beauty, evoked rapturous responses from both audiences and critics. It was something which had never been seen on the stage of the Art Theatre before and was never to be seen again. The production became a hymn to a bygone era of cultured sophistication, refined feeling, aesthetic extravagance and leisured grace – as well as its swansong. Dobuzhinski sought to convey the spirit of the era, not only in the extreme richness of his settings, but through the balance and symmetry within them which he found typical of the so-called 'Empire' style of the 1840s, and which symbolized a degree of balance and harmony within this staged reflection of an idealized past.

Acts 1 and 5 were set in a circular drawing room, the walls of which were painted dove grey. A dark-blue, flower-patterned cornice met a white-stuccoed ceiling, which had a heavy moulded surround. From the centre of the ceiling hung a gilded chandelier. In the centre of the rear wall was a tall, arched window, the same height as the room, draped with lace curtains, through which could be seen a view of the park which was part of the Islayev

'A Month in the Country'

estate. The parquet floor was tiled in highly polished, light brown wood with a large rose-pattern motif in the centre. Every other detail of the setting emphasized its balanced symmetry. Downstage left and right stood identical ornamental white marble arches, extending from floor to ceiling, in which stood identical white 'Grecian' urns. In front of the lower half of each were identical firescreens, with wooden surrounds and richly embroidered canvas centres. To right and left of the central window stood evenly spaced, low Doric columns set against the wall, on each of which stood a vase of red flowers. Under the window itself was a regency-style window seat with rich silk upholstery striped in blue and gold, with two matching settees placed against the rear wall on either side. In front of them were identical oval tables with elaborately wrought pedestals, covered with blue cloths and flanked by two sets of elegantly styled period chairs, all of Karelian birchwood. The wall decorations were equally symmetrical, from the gilt ornamental garlands spaced at regular intervals around the walls of the room to the small cameos and pictures. Facing each other, on the walls either side of the window, were two enormous paintings of the same size and proportions, one depicting a storm at sea, in typical Romantic style, the other a volcano erupting, executed in the style of Bryllov's famous painting, 'The Destruction of Pompeii'. The pictures were typical examples of the kind of thing popular at the time, while their particular subject matter seemed, to Dobuzhinski, to cast an ironic light on the calm of the estate and on Natalya Petrovna's expressed longing for a fresh wind to waft into her life. The park seen through the window looked less typical of the Russian countryside than of something designed and executed by Capability Brown, or like the planned symmetry of the parks in St Petersburg.

The images of the inhabitants of this 'nest of the gentry' were conveyed through the costumes which, in stylized 1840s fashion, fused organically with the setting. A critic described them as elegant and beautiful, as if the characters had stepped out of the frame of a painting by Simov or Borisov-Musatov. The least elaborate of the settings, such as the garden, suddenly became enlivened by the bright colours of Katya's yellow dress or Vera's red dress with black dots. Although Vera's dresses were said not to have suited the actress, all agreed that the colours and designs were delightful – from pink, to white, to one with blue checks.[8]

There is no doubt that Stanislavski saw Belyayev, fairly conventionally, as a positive force in the play and not in the ironic light which, it was suggested earlier, also formed part of Turgenev's intentions. The role was taken by the young Richard Boleslavski, dressed in typical student's uniform of the period, wearing a cap and with long, romantically flowing hair. There was great youthfulness and purity about his performance which had nothing 'actorish' about it. Rakitin, however, was the ruling idea of the production. As a later critic has declared:

> [Stanislavski] believed and steadfastly continued to declare from the stage that the Romantic spirit was alive. Perhaps it was old-fashioned and there were no longer any Rakitins in existence but the Rakitin spirit of knightly nobility would always continue to live with its spiritual delicacy and mild, patient selflessness.[9]

The ruling idea of the play related to the destruction of the epic quiet of the life of the nobility. The actors were to sit without moving and, through their inner feelings, reflected in their speech, were to infect the spectators with a

'A Month in the Country'

sense of the 'dialectic of the soul' from which nothing should distract their attention. Rakitin became the main philosophical link in the chain of the production, the true spiritual hero in a drama of the destruction of refined aestheticism and the repudiation of moral nobility.

To return briefly to the problems with which the play appears to pose a would-be interpreter, it is perhaps inevitable that, writing in the early 1850s, and out of a similar background, Turgenev was incapable of depicting the collapse of an aristocratic order in the equivalent terms of a Chekhov in *The Cherry Orchard*, where the accelerating social process appears to have had the effect of reducing the characters to caricatures. Nevertheless, implicit within Turgenev's consciousness, and partially enshrined in his dramatic method, is precisely this duality between the human and the grotesque, between psychological realism and puppetry, between romanticism and naturalism.

It is interesting that the problem appears to have been recognized by critics of English productions of the play, which have tended, like English productions of Chekhov, to anglicize the milieu and to present the characters in a sentimental and uncritically 'humanist' light. Reviewing Michael Redgrave's 1956 New York production with Uta Hagen and Luther Adler of Emlyn Williams's adaptation of the play, Eric Bentley praised the play's dramatic construction and the 'airy and consistent lightness, a liquid grace' of the conception.[10] However, in a later reflection on this production he became more critical, for instance, of what he saw to be Redgrave's presentation of Belyayev as 'non-intellectual' which he described in strong terms as 'an impertinence', stating that he thought the director had 'played up the funny side of the play so much that the sad side suffered'. While pointing out that: 'Mr. Redgrave has publicly defended his "comic" interpretation against the straw man of a "romantic" interpretation', Bentley put his finger on the problem, which it is clear Redgrave's production had been aware of, and, going against tradition, had sought to resolve more on the comic-grotesque side. However in Bentley's view, it was not in the sacrifice of romanticism that the production's fault lay but in its apparent inability to unite both aspects:

> . . . everything – every single thing – that we call either comic or romantic has to be *there* on stage. Neither must be sacrificed to the other.[11]

The play had earlier been presented during the 1949–50 season at the Old Vic in a fuller version than the Williams adaptation, with the soliloquies un-cut, directed by Michel St Denis. In her survey of Old Vic drama, Audrey Williamson complained that the director did not take Natalya Petrovna seriously, unlike Valerie Taylor's 1943 performance which was 'all neurotic vibration and pencil-drawn beauty . . . [with] more capacity for feeling pain than giving it'.[12] The scene of confession between Angela Baddeley as Natalya Petrovna, and Belyayev, was seen to disrupt the tone of the whole in being acted as 'melodramatic comedy', and Williamson concluded that:

> . . . one of the reasons for the play's comparatively poor success with audiences was probably this cleavage of style between comedy and drama, which made it difficult for them to judge just what their reaction should be or where they were.[13]

Again, this is precisely the difficulty which the play inherently presents and where convention requires that

'A Month in the Country'

the resolution be on a 'higher' plane of lyricism and psychological 'truth' to some permanently frozen conception of individualistically human 'character'.

The first British production of the full-length version of the play, although still with minor cuts, was given at the National Theatre, London, in February 1981, in a new translation by Isaiah Berlin, directed by Peter Gill and with Francesca Annis as Natalya Petrovna. Critics, generally, did not care for the production with its very expensive, abstract setting of greenish, dyed wood flooring and independently floating roof. This had the effect of emphasizing the large expanse of the stage in the Olivier Theatre, across which the actors were forced to shout. It was felt that Francesca Annis's stylized playing was excessively mannered and melodramatic, as if she had been misdirected, and that this clashed with other styles of acting within the production. However, all agreed that she looked very beautiful in dresses made from specially imported French material. The new translation was approved of, but the play was considered too long, and a boring production would have benefited, on this occasion, from judicious cutting. Interesting observations were made to the effect that Turgenev anticipated Ibsen and was even as avant-garde as Büchner.[14] One critic commended a connection which the production had sensed between Natalya Petrovna and Hedda Gabler, as well as between Turgenev and Marivaux.[15] Nevertheless, it is probably true to say, that Turgenev still awaits a good British production of *A Month in the Country* in its authentic entirety, as well as first performances of all his other, equally worthwhile, dramatic works.

Notes and References

1. Two Lives

1. Henri Troyat, *Gogol* (London: Allen & Unwin, 1974) p. 8.
2. I. S. Turgenev, *Literary Reminiscences* (London: Faber & Faber, 1959) p. 149.
3. Avrahm Yarmolinsky, *Turgenev: The Man, his Art and his Age* (London: Hodder & Stoughton, 1926) p. 95.
4. David Magarshack, *Gogol: A Life* (London: Faber & Faber, 1957) p. 271.
5. Turgenev, *Literary Reminiscences,* p. 142.

2. Two Worlds

1. N. V. Gogol, 'Petersburg Notes of 1836', *Russian Literature Triquarterly,* VII (Winter 1974) 178.
2. Isaiah Berlin, 'Birth of the Russian Intelligentsia', in H. Hardy and A. Kelly (eds) *Russian Thinkers* (Harmondsworth: Penguin Books, 1979) p. 11.
3. Yarmolinsky, *Turgenev* 102.
4. Berlin, 'Vissarion Belinsky', *Russian Thinkers,* p. 167.
5. Turgenev, *Literary Reminiscences,* p. 128.

Notes and References

6. Irving Howe, *Politics and the Novel* (New York: Avon Books, 1967) p. 121.
7. Donald Fanger, *The Creation of Nikolai Gogol* (Massachusetts: Harvard University Press, 1979) p. 146.
8. Marc Slonim, *An Outline of Russian Literature* (Oxford University Press, 1958) p. 87.
9. Vsevolod Setchkarev, *Gogol: His Life and Works* (London: Peter Owen, 1965) p. 122.
10. Simon Karlinsky, *The Sexual Labyrinth of Nikolai Gogol* (Massachusetts: Harvard University Press, 1976) pp. 26–7.

3. Theatrical Theories and Influences

1. B. V. Varneke, *History of the Russian Theatre* (New York: Hafner Publishing Co., 1971) p. 290.
2. Galina Vinnikova, *Turgenev i Rossiya* (Moscow: 'Sovetskaya Rossiya', 1977) p. 57.
3. Varneke, *Russian Theatre,* p. 295.
4. Nora Gottlieb and Raymond Chapman (eds), *Letters to an Actress: The Story of Turgenev and Savina* (London: Allison & Busby, 1973) p. 31.
5. Gogol, 'Petersburg Notes', 183.
6. Ibid., p. 184.
7. N. V. Gogol, 'After the Play', *Tulane Drama Review* (Winter, 1959) 183.
8. Ibid., 184.
9. James West, *Russian Symbolism* (London: Methuen, 1970) p. 141.
10. N. V. Gogol, 'On the Theater, On the One-Sided View Towards the Theater, and on One-Sidedness in General', *Selected Passages from Correspondence with Friends* (Nashville: Vanderbilt University Press, 1969) p. 75.
11. G. P. Berdnikov (ed), *Turgenev i Teatr* (Moscow: 'Iskusstvo', 1953) p. 56.
12. A. Anikst, *Teoriya Dramy v Rossii ot Pushkina do Chekhova* (Moscow: 'Nauka', 1972) p. 184.
13. Berdnikov, *Turgenev i Teatr* 93–8.
14. Ibid., p. 7.
15. Ibid., p. 33.
16. Ibid., p. 36.

17. Ibid., p. 20.
18. Gogol, *Selected Passages from Correspondence with Friends,* pp. 79–80.

4. Gogol's Plays 1832–1842

1. Janko Lavrin, *Nikolai Gogol* (London: Sylvan Press, 1951) p. 79.
2. S. S. Danilov, *Gogol' i Teatr* (Leningrad: 'Khudozhestvennaya Literatura', 1936) p. 68.
3. Varneke, *Russian Theatre* 314.
4. Eric Bentley, 'Gogol's Gaiety' – Notes on *The Marriage, A Madman's Diary* and *Gamblers* (Yale/Theatre 1976) p. 12.
5. N. V. Gogol', *Sobranie Khudozhestvennykh Proyzvedenii,* 5 vols (Collected Works), vol. IV ed. with notes by I. N. Medvedeva (Moscow: Izd. 'Akademii Nauk CCCP', 1959) see note p. 461.
6. Ibid., p. 461
7. Fanger, *Nikolai Gogol,* see note 7, p. 287.
8. William Woodin Rowe, *Through Gogol's Looking Glass* (New York University Press, 1976) p. 148.
9. Karlinsky, *Sexual Labyrinth,* 282.
10. Inna Vishnevskaya, 'O Chom Napisana Zhenit'ba?', *Teatr,* 1 (1973) pp. 98–112.
11. Frantisek Deak, 'The Influence of Italian Futurism in Russia', *The Drama Review,* XIX, 4 (T-68 Dec. 1975) 92.
12. Danilov, *Gogol i Teatr* 240–1.
13. Nikolai A. Gorchakov, *The Theatre in Soviet Russia* (New York: Columbia University Press, 1957) p. 339.
14. For definitions of this useful term, which is generally translated as 'banality' or 'vulgarity', see Vladimir Nabokov, *Nikolai Gogol* (New York: New Directions, 1961) pp. 63–74 and D. S. Mirsky, *A History of Russian Literature* (New York: Vintage Books, 1958) p. 158.
15. Danilov, *Gogol i Teatr,* 214.
16. Maria Szewcow, 'The Theatre of Anatolij Efros', *Theatre Quarterly,* VII, 26 (1977) 41.

5. 'The Government Inspector'

1. Troyat, *Gogol* 135.

Notes and References

2. Turgenev, *Literary Reminiscences,* p. 145.
3. Varneke, *Russian Theatre,* 308.
4. Victor Erlich, *Gogol* (New Haven: Yale University Press, 1969) p. 107.
5. Anikst, *Teoriya Dramy,* 164–7.
6. Ibid., pp. 137–40.
7. Gogol, *Collected Works,* p. 144.
8. Boris Alpers, *Aktyorskoe Iskusstvo v Rossii* (Moscow/Leningrad: 'Iskusstvo', 1945) p. 259.
9. Dmitry Merezhkovsky, 'Gogol and the Devil', in Robert Maguire (ed.), *Gogol from the Twentieth Century* (New Jersey: Princeton University Press, 1974) p. 73.
10. Ibid., p. 60.
11. Vyacheslav Ivanov, 'Gogol's *Inspector General* and the Comedy of Aristophanes' in *Gogol from the Twentieth Century,* p. 201.
12. Vasily Gippius, *'The Inspector General:* Structure and Problems' in *Gogol from the Twentieth Century,* pp. 236–7.
13. Vladimir Nabokov, *Nikolai Gogol* (New York: New Directions, 1961) p. 42.
14. A. de Jonge, 'Gogol', in John Fennell (ed.), *Nineteenth-Century Russian Literature* (London: Faber & Faber, 1973) pp. 106–117.
15. N. V. Gogol, 'An Author's Confession', *Russian Literature Triquarterly,* x (Fall 1974) 106.
16. See N. Worrall, 'Meyerhold Directs Gogol's *Government Inspector', Theatre Quarterly,* II, 7 (Jul–Sep 1972) 75–95.
17. M. N. Stroeva, *Rezhissyorskie Iskaniya Stanislavskogo,* 1898–1917 (Moscow: 'Nauka', 1973) pp. 238–42.
18. V. Gromov, *Mikhail Chekhov* (Moscow: 'Iskusstvo', 1970) pp. 87–99.
19. Stroeva, *Rezhissyorskie Iskaniya Stanislavskogo,* 1917–1938 (Moscow: 'Nauka', 1977) pp. 50–68.
20. Danilov, *Gogol i Teatr* 259–62.
21. Audrey Williamson, *Old Vic Drama 2* (London: Rockliff, 1957) p. 9.
22. Gogol, *Collected Works,* see note p. 460.

6. Turgenev's Plays 1834–1848

1. N. A. Nekrasov, *'Kholostyak,* Komediya v Tryokh

Deystviyakh Iv. Turgeneva', in K. I. Bonetski (ed.), *Turgenev v Russkoy Kritike* (Moscow: 'Khudozhestvennaya Literatura', 1953) p. 106.
2. I. S. Turgenev, *Stikhotvoreniya i Poemy,* ed. I. Yampol'ski (Leningrad: 'Sovetskii Pisatel', 1970) see note p. 425.
3. Galina Vinnikova, 'Teatr Turgeneva', *Teatr,* XI (1968) 113.
4. V. G. Belinski, 'Parasha', *Turgenev v Russkoy Kritike,* p. 82.
5. Vinnikova, *Turgenev i Rossiya,* p. 73.

7. Turgenev's Plays 1848–1850

1. Berdnikov, 35.
2. P. A. Markov, *O Teatre* (4 vols), vol. III (Moscow: 'Iskusstvo', 1976) p.217.
3. Marc Slonim, *Russian Theater from the Empire to the Soviets* (London: Methuen, 1963) p. 67.
4. K. S. Stanislavski, *Moya Zhizn' v Iskusstve* (Moscow: 'Iskusstvo', 1962) pp. 508–11.
5. A. D. Diki, *Povest' o Teatral'noy Yunosti* (Moscow: 'Iskusstvo', 1957) p. 152.
6. Leonid Grossman, *Teatr Turgeneva* (Petersburg: Brokgaus-Yefron, 1924) p. 136.

8. 'A Month in the Country'

1. I. S. Turgenev, *Sobranie Sochinenii,* 12 vols, eds M. P. Alekseev and G. Byaly, vol. 9–10 notes and comments by Yu. P. Rybakova (Moscow: 'Khudozhestvennaya Literatura', 1979) p. 561.
2. Leonard Schapiro, *Turgenev: His Life and Times* (Oxford University Press, 1978) p. 76.
3. Richard Freeborn, *Turgenev: The Novelist's Novelist* (Oxford University Press, 1970) pp. 32–3.
4. Michael Redgrave, Introduction to *A Month in the Country* (London: Heinemann, 1953) p. ix.
5. Ibid., p. xiv.
6. See Edward Braun, *Meyerhold on Theatre* (London: Methuen, 1969), pp. 28–9, for the Russian director's view of the play as 'puppet show' and, pp. 33–4, his letter to Chekhov

Notes and References

expressing his opinion of the play's 'abstract' quality.

7. Constantin Stanislavski, *My Life in Art* (Harmondsworth: Penguin Books, 1967) pp. 499–500.

8. Grossman, *Teatr Turgeneva* 150-66.

9. Stroeva, *Rezhissyorskie Iskaniya,* 1898–1917, 252.

10. Eric Bentley, *What is Theatre?* (Boston: Beacon Press, 1956) p. 144.

11. Ibid., p. 230.

12. Williamson, *Old Vic Drama 2,* 41.

13. Ibid., p. 43.

14. James Fenton, 'Turgenev: a passion for reality', *The Sunday Times* (22 Feb 1981).

15. Robert Cushman, 'Acting your Age', *The Observer* (22 Feb 1981).

Bibliography

Alpers B., *Aktyorskoe Iskusstvo v Rossii* (1 vol. only) (Moscow/Leningrad: 'Iskusstvo', 1945).

Anikst A., *Teoriya Dramy v Rossii ot Pushkina do Chekhova* (Moscow: 'Nauka', 1972).

Belinski V. G., 'Letter to N. V. Gogol', in Ralph E. Matlaw (ed.) *Belinsky, Chernyshevsky, and Dobrolyubov – Selected Criticism* (New York: Dutton & Co., 1962).

Bentley E., *What is Theatre?* (Boston: Beacon Press, 1956).

Bentley E., Notes on *The Marriage, A Madman's Diary* and *Gamblers* (Yale/Theatre, 1976).

Berdnikov G. (ed.), *Turgenev i Teatr* (Moscow: 'Iskusstvo', 1953).

Berlin I., *Russian Thinkers* (Harmondsworth: Penguin Books, 1979).

Bonetski K. I. (ed.), *Turgenev v Russkoy Kritike* (Moscow: 'Khudozhestvennaya Literatura', 1953).

Brang P., *I. S. Turgenev: Sein Leben und sein Werk* (Wiesbaden: Otto Harrassowitz, 1977).

Burgess M. A. S., 'The Early Russian Theatre' in *Companion to Russian Studies* (3 vols) vol. 2, 'Introduction to Russian Language and Literature', eds. R. Auty and D. Obolensky (Cambridge University Press, 1977).

Bibliography

Danilov S. S., *Ocherki po Istorii Russkogo Dramaticheskogo Teatra* (Moscow/Leningrad: 'Iskusstvo', 1948).

Danilov S. S., *Gogol' i Teatr* (Leningrad: 'Khudozhestvennaya Literatura', 1936).

Diki A. D., *Povest' o Teatral'noy Yunosti* (Moscow: 'Iskusstvo', 1957).

Erlich V., *Gogol* (New Haven: Yale University Press, 1969).

Fanger D., *The Creation of Nikolai Gogol* (Massachusetts: Harvard University Press, 1979).

Freeborn R., *Turgenev: The Novelist's Novelist* (Oxford University Press, 1970).

Gifford H., 'Turgenev', in John Fennell (ed.) *Nineteenth-Century Russian Literature* (London: Faber & Faber, 1973).

Gippius V., *Gogol'* (Leningrad: 'Mysl', 1924), Brown University Press Slavic Reprint Series No. I (Provincetown, 1963).

Gogol' N. V., *Sobranie Khudozhestvennykh Proyzvedenii* (5 vols.) (Moscow: Izd. 'Akademii Nauk CCCP', 1959).

Gogol N. V., 'An Author's Confession', trans D. Lapeza, *Russian Literature Triquarterly,* x (Fall, 1974).

Gogol N. V., *Selected Passages from Correspondence with Friends* trans. J. Zeldin (Nashville: Vanderbilt University Press 1969).

Gogol N. V., 'Petersburg Notes of 1836', trans. L. Germano, *Russian Literature Triquarterly* VII (Winter, 1974).

Gorchakov N. A., *The Theatre in Soviet Russia* (New York: Columbia University Press, 1957).

Gottlieb N. and Chapman R., *Letters to an Actress: The Story of Turgenev and Savina* (London: Allison & Busby, 1973).

Gourfinkel N., *Nicolas Gogol – Dramaturge* (Paris: l'Arche, 1956).

Grossman L., *Teatr Turgeneva* (Petersburg: Brokgaus-Yefron, 1924).

Grossman L., 'On Turgenev', in A. Field (ed.), *The Complection of Russian Literature* (Harmondsworth: Penguin Books, 1971).

Hope-Wallace P., 'A Month in the Country', in Lionel Hale, *The Old Vic 1949–50* (London: Evans Bros, 1950).

Howe I., *Politics and the Novel* (New York: Avon Books, 1967).

Jonge A. de, 'Gogol', in J. Fennell (ed.), *Nineteenth-Century Russian Literature* (London: Faber & Faber, 1973).

Nikolai Gogol and Ivan Turgenev

Karlinsky S., *The Sexual Labyrinth of Nikolai Gogol* (Massachusetts: Harvard University Press, 1976).

Kott J., 'The Eating of *The Government Inspector*', *Theatre Quarterly*, v, 17 (1975).

Kropotkin P., *Russian Literature: Ideals and Realities* (London: Duckworth, 1916).

Kurlyanskaya G. B., *I. S. Turgenev i Russkaya Literatura* (Moscow: 'Prosveshchenie', 1980).

Lavrin J., *Nikolai Gogol* (London: Sylvan Press, 1951).

Lindstrom T. S., *Nikolay Gogol* (New York: Twayne Publishers Inc., 1974).

Magarshack D., *Gogol: A Life* (London: Faber & Faber, 1957).

Magarshack D., *Turgenev: A Life* (London: Faber & Faber, 1954).

Maguire R. (ed.), *Gogol from the Twentieth Century* (New Jersey: Princeton University Press, 1976).

Mirsky D. S., *A History of Russian Literature*, ed. F. J. Whitfield (New York: Vintage Books, 1958).

Nabokov V., *Nikolai Gogol* (New York: New Directions, 1961).

Pritchett V. S., *The Gentle Barbarian: The Life and Work of Turgenev* (London: Chatto & Windus, 1977).

Rahv P., 'Gogol as a Modern Instance', in D. Davie (ed.) *Russian Literature and Modern English Fiction* (Chicago University Press, 1965).

Revyakin A. I., *Istoriya Russkoy Literatury 19ogo Veka* (Pervaya Polovina) (Moscow: 'Prosveshchenie', 1977).

Rowe W. W., *Through Gogol's Looking Glass* (New York University Press, 1976).

Schapiro L., *Turgenev – His Life and Times* (Oxford University Press, 1978).

Setchkarev V., *Gogol: His Life and Works*, trans. R. Kramer (London: Peter Owen, 1965).

Simmons E. J., *Introduction to Russian Realism* (Bloomington: Indiana University Press, 1965).

Slonim M., *The Epic of Russian Literature* (New York: Oxford University Press, 1964).

Slonim M., *Russian Theatre from the Empire to the Soviets* (London: Methuen, 1961).

Slonim M., *An Outline of Russian Literature* (Oxford University Press 1958).

Bibliography

Stanislavski K., *Moya Zhizn' v Iskusstve* (Moscow: 'Iskusstvo', 1962).

Stanislavski C., *My Life in Art* (Harmondsworth: Penguin Books, 1967).

Stepanova N. L. (ed.), *Gogol' i Teatr* (Moscow: 'Iskusstvo', 1952).

Stroeva M. S., *Rezhissyorskie Iskaniya Stanislavskogo,* 1898–1917 (Moscow: 'Nauka', 1973).

────────── *Rezhissyorskie Iskaniya Stanislavskogo,* 1917-38 (Moscow: 'Nauka', 1977).

Troyat H., *Gogol,* trans. N. Amphoux (London: Allen & Unwin, 1974).

Turgenev I.S., *Sobranie Sochinenii* (12 vols), vol. 9-10 'Tseny i Komedii', eds. M. P. Alekseev and G. A. Byaly (Moscow: 'Khudozhestvennaya Literatura', 1979).

Turgenev I. S., *Stikhotvorenie i Poemy,* ed. I. Yampol'ski (Leningrad: 'Sovetskii Pisatel'', 1970).

Turgenev I. S., *Turgenev's Literary Reminiscences,* translated and with an introduction by D. Magarshack (London: Faber & Faber, 1959).

Varneke B. V., *History of the Russian Theatre,* trans. B. Brasol, revised and edited by B. Martin (New York: Hafner Publishing Co., 1971).

Vinogradskaya I., *Zhizn' i Tvorchestvo K. S. Stanislavskogo* (4 vols) vol 2 1906–15 (Moscow: 'VTO', 1971), vol 3 1916–26 (Moscow: 'VTO', 1973).

Vinnikova G., *Turgenev i Rossiya* (Moscow: 'Sovetskaya Rossiya', 1977).

Vishnevskaya I. L., *Gogol' i ego Komedii* (Moscow: 'Nauka', 1976).

Williamson A., *Old Vic Drama 2* (London: Rockliff, 1957).

Williamson A., *Theatre of Two Decades* (London: Rockliff, 1951).

Yarmolinsky A., *Turgenev: The Man, his Art and his Age* (London: Hodder & Stoughton, 1926).

Zolotusski I., *Gogol'* (Moscow: 'Molodaya Gvardiya', 1979).

Editions of the Plays of Gogol and Turgenev in Translation

The Collected Tales and Plays of Nikolay Gogol, translated by Constance Garnett, revised and edited with an introduction and notes by Leonard J. Kent (New York: Octagon Books, 1978).

The Theatre of Nikolay Gogol – Plays and Selected Writings, with an introduction and notes by Milton Ehre, translated by M. Ehre and F. Gottschalk (Chicago University Press, 1980).

There have been several translations of *The Government Inspector.* Among the most recent, and more widely available, are the 'acting version' by Edward O. Marsh and Jeremy Brooks (London: Eyre Methuen, 1968) and the more literal rendering by Joshua Cooper translated as *The Inspector* in *Four Russian Plays,* translated with an introduction by Joshua Cooper, (Harmondsworth: Penguin Books, 1972).

There have been a few translations and 'acting versions' of *Marriage* and *Gamblers.* Notable among the latter have been those of Eric Bentley in vols 3 and 5 of *The Modern Theatre,* ed. E. Bentley (New York: Doubleday Anchor, 1955). The most widely available translation of *Marriage* is that of Bella Costello (Manchester University Press, 1969).

The Plays of Ivan S. Turgenev, translated by M. S. Mandell with

Plays of Gogol and Turgenev in Translations

an introduction by William Lyon Phelps (New York: Russell & Russell, 1970) is a reissue of the 1924 Macmillan edition.

Ivan Turgenev: Three Plays: (A Month in the Country, A Provincial Lady, A Poor Gentleman), translated by Constance Garnett (AMS Press, 1976 and Hyperion, Conn., 1977) are reissues of the 1951 Duckworth edition which was itself a reissue of the 1934 Cassell edition.

Generally available editions of *A Month in the Country* are the 'acting version' by Emlyn Williams, with an introduction by Michael Redgrave (London: Heinemann Educational Books, 1976), and a translation by Ariadne Nicolaeff specially prepared for the 1974 Chichester Festival Theatre production, with an introduction by the director, Toby Robertson (London: Samuel French, 1976).

Index

Adler, Luther 185
'Affair of the 32' 14
Aksakov, S. T. 89
Alexander I, Tsar 19
Alexander II, Tsar 13
Alexei Mikhailovich, Tsar 34
Alfred the Great 20, 57
Anarchist Movement 8
Ancient Greece 18, 21–2, 26; 5th-century Athens 43
Andreyev, Leonid, *The Life of Man* 107
Androsov, V. 86–7, 113
Annenkov, P. V. 11
Annis, Francesca 187
Aristophanes 42, 46

Baddeley, Angela 186
Bakunin, A. A. 118
Bakunin, Mikhail 8, 10, 14, 24
Bakunin, Tatyana 8
Balzac 27

Bardach, Emilie 16
Bebutov, V. 110
Beckett, Samuel 72, 99
Belinski, V. G. 8, 10, 22, 23, 38, 45, 66, 86, 87, 88, 113, 121; *Letter to Gogol* 10
Bell, The (*Kolokol*) 13, 14
Bentley, Eric 61, 185–6
Berlin 8; University of 21
Berlin, Isaiah 187
Boileau 32
Boleslavski, Richard 184
Borisov-Musatov, V. 184
Brecht, Bertolt 59; *The Resistible Rise of Arturo Ui* 100
Browning, Robert 14
Bryantsev, A. A. 79
Büchner, Georg 187
Bulgarin, F. 66, 113
Burrell, John 112
Byron 118

Index

Calderon 21, 39; *El Magico Prodigioso* 39; *Life is a Dream* 21, 39
Cambridge, *Festival Theatre* 176
Campbell, D. J. 112
Carlyle, Thomas 13
Catherine, Empress 18, 19
Cervantes, *Don Quixote* 13, 22, 131
Chekhov, Anton 68, 170–1, 173; *The Cherry Orchard* 180, 185; *The Proposal* 157; *Three Sisters* 171; *Uncle Vanya* 176
Chekhov, Michael 106, 108–10
Chernyshevski, N. G. 57, 88
Chichester, *Festival Theatre* 179
Commedia dell'Arte 32, 103, 178, 182
The Contemporary 9, 49 139, 158, 171
Corneille 32
Courtavenel 39

Daudet, Alphonse 14
Davydov, V. N. 106, 140, 141–2
de Maupassant, Guy 14
Dickens, Charles 13, 14, 154; *Household Words* 13
Diderot 39
Diki, A. D. 167
Disraeli, Benjamin 13
Dobuzhinski, M. V. 168–9, 182–4
Dostoevski, Fyodor 10, 15, 16, 20, 24, 67, 68, 142; *Crime and Punishment* 15; *The Double* 68; *The Possessed* 16
Dyur, N. O. 106

Edinburgh 14; Edinburgh Festival 80
Efros, Anatoli 80, 174
Efros, N. E. 169
Eisenstein, Sergei 77
Eliot, George 14
Elizaveta Petrovna, Empress 32
Expressionism 79, 103

FEKS 77
Feminist Movement 121
Flaubert, Gustave 14
Fonvizin, Denis 33, 39; *The Brigadier* 33; *The Minor* 33
France 10, 18, 117, 139; French Revolution 18; Paris 10, 14, 15, 16, 24, 39; Paris Commune 14
Freeborn, Richard 173
Futurist Movement (Russian) 77, 104

Gaideburov Travelling Popular Theatre 79
Garin, Erast 103
Garnett, Constance 58, 173
Gedeonov, S. A. 44; *The Death of Lyapunov* 44–5
Gerzhenson, M. O. 118
Gill, Peter 187
Gippius, V. 90
Giraud, Giovanni, *The Embarrassed Uncle* 40
Goethe 22; *Faust* 45–6
Gogol, M. I. 2, 3, 4

Index

Gogol, N. V.: LIFE 1–16; WORKS: *Advance Notice To Those Wishing To Act The Government Inspector Properly* 42, 87, 101; *Alfred* 6, 55–8; *An Author's Confession* 90; *Arabesques* 7, 55; *Conversation After The Play (Upon Leaving The Theatre After The Performance Of A New Comedy)* 41–2, 87, 113–15; *Dead Souls* 2, 7, 8, 9, 11, 13, 22, 27, 55, 66, 67, 127; *The Dénouement of the Government Inspector* 91; *The Diary of a Madman* 5, 49, 65, 142; *Evenings on a Farm Near Dikanka* 5; *Gamblers* 9, 28, 58–65, 73, 88, 103; *The Government Inspector (Revizor)* 7, 8, 16, 28, 34, 35, 47, 58, 71, 73, 81–113, 158; *Hanz Kuechelgarten* 5; *Marriage (The Suitors, The Provincial Suitor)* 2, 8, 9, 28, 48, 58, 66–80, 88, 110, 131, 134; *Mirgorod* 7; *Old World Landowners* 4; *The Order of Vladimir, Third Class* 48–55 (*Morning of a Man of Affairs* 49–50, *The Lawsuit* 50–1, *The Servants' Hall* 51–3, 144, *Scenes from High Society* 53–5); *The Overcoat* 5, 142; *Selected Passages from Correspondence with Friends* 9, 10, 25; *The Shaved-Off Moustache* 6, 55; *Taras Bulba* 55, 58; *Treatise on Woman* 26

Gogol, V. A. 2; *The Simpleton* 36; *The Tricks of a Woman Outwitted by a Soldier* 36

Goncharov, I. 10, 20

Goncourt, E. de 14

Gorky, Maxim 33

Goryev, A. 108

Greek Orthodox Church 31; *The Burning Fiery Furnace* 31

Gregori, Johann Gottfried 31

Griboyedov, Alexander 33; *Woe from Wit (The Misfortune of Being Clever/Chatski)* 34, 37

Grigoryev, Apollon 79

Guinness, Alec 112

Hagen, Uta 185

Hall, Anmer 176

Hall, Peter 112, 113

Hallam, *Europe in the Middle Ages* 55

Hegel, Friedrich 8, 21, 22, 23, 132

Herzen, Alexander 10, 13, 14, 24, 25, 37, 130

Homer 22

Hugo, Victor 14

Ibsen, Henrik 16, 124, 163–4, 179, 187; *A Doll's House* 163–4, 167; *Hedda Gabler* 163–4, 165, 167, 179–80, 187; *Rosmersholm* 163–4

Imperial Theatres 5, 38

Ionesco, Eugene 76

Index

Isakov, S. P. 79
Ivanov, Vyacheslav 43, 89–90

James, Henry 15
Jefford, Barbara 113
Jonge, A. de 90
Jonson, Ben, *The Alchemist* 59; *Volpone* 59

Kachalov, V. 130
Kapnist, V. V., *The Slanderer* 34
Karatygina, A. M. 129
Karpov, E. P. 110
Khrapovitski 84
Kiev, University of 5
Knipper, Olga 130
Knyazhnin, Ya. B. 34
Koni, F. A. 36
Konstantinovski, Father Matthew 11
Kotlyarevski, N. A. 58
Kotzebue 32
Kozintsev, Grigori 77
Krylov, I. A. 35; *A Lesson for Daughters* 35
Kukolnik, N. V. 44; *Commissioner-General Patkul* 44–5

Lazarenko, V. 78
Leningrad, Gorky Theatre 113; Press House 111
Lenski, D. T. 87, 106
Lermontov, Mikhail 10, 20; *Masquerade* 37, 103
Lessing 39, 40; *Emilia Galotti* 124
Livings, Henry 112
London 13, 14, 15; Aldwych Theatre 112; National Theatre 187; New Theatre 112; St James's Theatre 173
London, Jack, *The Mexican* 78
Lunacharski, Anatoli 104

Macaulay, T. B. 13
Malibran 3
Mandell, M. S. 159
Marivaux 187
Markov, Pavel 141
Martynov, A. E. 79
Mayakovski, Vladimir 104; *Mystery-Bouffe* 78
Mazon, André 118
Melodrama 32, 37, 40, 44–5, 124
Merezhkovski, Dmitri 88, 90; *Gogol and the Devil* 88, 103
Mérimée, Prosper 15; *The Devil Woman* 119; *The Theatre of Clara Gazul* 119, 120
Meyerhold, V. E. 47, 77, 78, 102–105, 168; State Theatre Workshop 77
Miles, Bernard 112
Mitchell, Adrian 112
Molière 32, 33, 36, 39, 40, 86, 121; *Critique of the School for Wives* 113; *The Imaginary Invalid* 40; *Tartuffe* 40
Monakhov, I. I. 106
Morris, William 20
Moscow 10, 38, 66; Red Square 32; Moscow Art Theatre 38, 47, 78, 106,

Index

130, 141, 167, 170, 180;
Malaya Bronnaya Theatre
80; Maly Theatre 37, 141,
172 ; Sovremennik Theatre
112; Trades Union Theatre
110; Bolshoi Theatre 141;
Proletkult Theatre 77–8
Moscow News 12
Moscow Observer 86
Moskvin, Ivan 108
Mozart, *Don Giovanni* 121
Musset, Alfred de 129, 138;
Un Caprice 129

Nabokov, Vladimir 88, 90
Napoleon 19
'The Natural School' 125
Nature, Gogol's and
Turgenev's attitudes
towards 26, 29
Nekrasov, N. A. 10, 116
Nemirovich-Danchenko, V. 168
Nicholas I, Tsar 7, 13, 19, 24, 84, 85
The Northern Bee 66
Notes of the Fatherland 162

'October in the Theatre'
movement 104
Oedipus Rex 59
Oldekop 82
Ostrovski, Alexander,
Balzaminov Trilogy 68;
Enough Stupidity in Every Wise Man 78; *A Lucrative Post* 68; *It's a Family Affair* 10, 46
Oxford, University of 15

Patriotic Institute 5

Peter the Great 17, 18, 28, 32, 57
Petrashevski circle 24
Petrov, N. V. 110
Plato 86, 94
Pletnyov, P. A. 7
Polevoy, N. 85
Potato Theatre 39
Potyomkin, P., *Petrushka* 168
Pravda 141
Pre-Raphaelites 20
Prokopovich, N. Ya 113
Prospect Theatre Company 113
Pugachov Rebellion 18
Puppet show 36, 163, 165, 168; *vertep* 36
Pushkin, Alexander 7, 8, 15, 19, 40, 49, 81, 82; *Boris Godunov* 37; *Eugene Onegin* 8, 19, 130; *The Stone Guest* 108

Racine 32, 39
Rastrelli 28, 134
Redgrave, Michael 174, 176, 185–6
Revue des études slaves 118
Richardson, Ian 113
Robertson, Toby 113, 179
Rogers, Paul 112
Romanticism 119, 183, 184, 186
Rossetti, D. G. 14
Ruskin, John 20
Russian Orthodox Church 9, 25

Sadovski, M. P. 106
Sadovski, Prov 106

Index

Saltykov-Shchedrin, M. 68
Samarin, I. V. 106
Samoilova, V. V. 129
Sand, George 15
Savina, Marya 16, 39, 172
Saxe-Meiningen Company 107
Schapiro, Leonard 173
Schiller, Friedrich 40, 45; *William Tell* 45
Scofield, Paul 112
Scott, Sir Walter, centenary celebrations 14
Scribe, Eugene 46
Senkovski, O. 85, 113
Serge and Taurek 78
Shakespeare 22, 32, 39, 138; *Hamlet* 13, 22, 39, 130, 131; *Henry IV Pt 2* 152; *King Lear* 7; *Othello* 7
Shakhovskoy, Prince A. A. 33
Shchepkin, M. S. 33, 36–7, 58, 85, 87, 106, 117, 139, 141, 148
Sheffield, *Crucible Theatre* 112–13
Shumski, S. V. 106
Sizov, N. I. 79
skomorokh 31
Slavophile/Westernizer Debate 25
Slonim, Marc 142
Somov, K. 184
Socrates 86, 94
Sosnitski, I. I. 66, 84, 106
Spasskoye (Oryol) 2, 10
St Denis, Michel 186
St Petersburg 5, 9, 12, 13, 14, 15, 16, 28, 29, 32, 38, 66; Alexandrinski Theatre 7, 35, 38, 84, 105, 130, 141, 148, 158; Marinski Theatre 114; University of 3, 6; Volkovo Cemetery 16
Stanislavski, Konstantin 37, 106–10, 167–9, 170, 180–5; *My Life In Art* 168, 181
Stankevich, N. V. 8, 22
Strindberg, August 176, 179; *A Dream Play* 120; *The Ghost Sonata* 75
Sukhovo-Kobylin, Alexander 68
Sumarokov, Alexander 32, 33, 38
Swinburne, Algernon 14
Symbolist Movement 43, 79, 103, 163, 182

Tabakov, Oleg 112
Table of Ranks 18, 28
Taylor, Valerie 186
Terentyev, I. 111
Thackeray, W. M. 13
Tolstoy, Leo 12, 15; *Anna Karenina* 15; *War and Peace* 15
Topolski, F. 112
Tovstonogov, Georgi 113
Trauberg, Leonid 77
Tsitsiyanov, Prince, *The Real Government Inspector* 84
Turgenev, Ivan: LIFE 1–16; WORKS: *The Bachelor* 9, 29, 116, 148–57, 159; *The Brigadier* 3; *Conversation on the High Road* 116; *Diary of a Superfluous Man* 130; *Evening in Sorrento* 116; *Fathers and Sons* 2, 13, 29, 175, 177; *A Hunter's*

206

Index

Sketches 9, 12, 13, 24, 29; *Indiscretion* 35, 116, 119, 120–4; *Literary Reminiscences* 8; *Lunch with the Marshal of the Nobility* 36, 116, 157–162; *Moneyless (Scenes From the Petersburg Life of a Young Nobleman)* 9, 36, 116, 125–9, 157; *A Month in the Country (The Student/ Two Women)* 16, 29, 39, 47, 116, 117, 123, 168, 170–87; *My Mates Sent Me* 10; *A Nest of Gentlefolk (Liza)* 13, 175; *On The Eve* 13, 175, 178; *Parasha* 8, 121; *The Parasite (Alien Bread)* 2, 29, 116, 117, 134, 139–48, 149, 159; *A Provincial Lady* 116, 162–9; *Rudin* 13, 118, 175; *Smoke* 16; *Styeno* 7, 116, 117–18; *The Temptation of St Antony* 116, 118–20; *Two Sisters* 119; *Virgin Soil* 12, 15; *Where It's Thin, There It Breaks* 116, 123, 129–38, 139, 167
Turgenev, Nikolai 3, 15, 172
Turgenev, S. N. 2, 3

Turgenev, V. P. 2, 3, 10

Ukraine 55; Sorochintsy (Poltava) 2; Gogol's planned history of 6
Uralov, I. M. 106

Vaudeville 35, 82, 97, 98, 113, 125, 157, 162
Velgorski, Count 83
Viardot, Louis 16
Viardot-Garcia, Pauline 3, 8, 10, 16, 27, 39, 46
Vishnevskaya, Inna 67
Voices of the Past 118
Volkov, Fyodor 32
Voltaire 18
Vyazemski, Prince 83, 84, 86, 113

Williams, Emlyn 173, 185
Williamson, Audrey 186
Woman, Theme of 26–7

Yablochkin, A. A. 105
Yermakov, I. 111

Zavadski, Yuri 78–9
Zhukovski, V. A. 83
Zola, Emile 14
Zubrov, P. I. 105